# From Sticks and Stones

*The Evolution of Golf Equipment Rules*

# Frank Thomas
with
Valerie Melvin

FRANKLY

Frankly Publications
Reunion, Florida

This book is dedicated to the two organizations for which I have the utmost respect and which have been a significant part of my life. Without the USGA and R&A the game would be rudderless and mankind would suffer.

To The United States Golf Association

and

The Royal and Ancient Golf Club of St. Andrews

Thank you for giving me the opportunity to serve the game I love so much.

**FRANKLY**

A Frankly Publication
Reunion Resort and Club
7593 Gathering Drive
Reunion, Florida 34747

Published throughout the world by Frankly Publications

ISBN: 9780615461717

Frankly Publications are available for group discounts and premium editions. For more information, contact Frankly Publications, 7593 Gathering Drive, Reunion, FL 34747, or via email at www.franklygolf.com.

Cover Image: Iain Lowe Photography
Designed by Pam Pollack.
Printed in the United States of America.
First edition.
Sponsored by the Acushnet Company
The views expressed in this book are those of the authors and are not attributable to any sponsor.

Excerpts from *The Rules of Golf* are reprinted from *The Rules of Golf 2010-2011* ©2009 United States Golf Association, with permission. All rights reserved.

*The Rules of Golf*, which were effective as of January 1, 2010, will remain current until they are next revised effective January 1, 2012. Readers should refer to the full text of the Rules in the official publications, *The Rules of Golf* and *The Decisions on the Rules of Golf*, which are published by the United States Golf Association and R&A Rules Limited.

This publication summarizes some of *The Rules of Golf* as interpreted by the author. The United States Golf Association does not warrant the accuracy of the author's interpretations.

The United States Golf Association is the Governing Authority for the *Rules of Golf* for the USA and Mexico; R&A Rules Limited is the Governing Authority for the *Rules of Golf* for the rest of the world.

# CONTENTS

# ACKNOWLEDGMENTS

To my co-author Valerie Melvin a great Scottish golfer and researcher in her own right, who did so much of the ground work, and to Jeff Neuman for his golf knowledge, his research time and his magic pen that turns disjointed thoughts into readable prose, my sincere thanks.

To some other good souls such as Rand Jerris and his staff at the USGA Museum, and to Peter Lewis, former Director of the British Golf Museum, I thank you for your input and for allowing us access to the history files.

Without Wally Uihlein of the Acushnet Company, and his belief that some things of importance deserve to be documented, this book would never have been written. Thank you for giving me the opportunity.

# INTRODUCTION

There is something warm and comforting about a den of constancy in our lives when everything around us is changing so fast. We are bombarded with daily updates of innovations that will improve our lifestyle by providing more information in a shorter period of time or making it faster and more comfortable for us to get to places we may not even want to go.

It was in 1908 – practically antediluvian in today's time scales – that the first equipment regulations were formulated and included in the Rules of Golf, which themselves were formally documented in 1744, 164 years earlier.

The 1744 Rules of Golf – which were probably used for a hundred years or more prior to their formal adoption – are fundamentally the same as those we use today and are the code that lends order to our game. As in life, we need rules to guide us and to prevent misunderstandings, and those rules will change over time, but the principles underlying them have remained largely in place.

This degree of constancy in the rules governing golf is remarkable when we consider the pace of progress in the surrounding world. It was in 1903 that we were first able to fly in airplanes, and in less than seventy years we reached the moon. Technology has engulfed us in exponential proportions, but we continue to enjoy and crave our time on a golf course. The activity must fulfill an important subconscious urge – our need to test and evaluate ourselves – if it has survived so long with so little change.

In the first half of the twentieth century, many rules changes were based on anecdotal evidence or fear that products of the mechanical age might rob the game of its intrinsic challenge. Some changes stemmed from an executive's personal view that something had to be done to solve a problem or a perceived problem. These impulses are all too human and have survived our transition to the age of research and development.

Scientific principles entered the design and development of golf equipment in the mid 1960s, and this trend increased fairly rapidly – though not when compared to other walks of life – until the early 2000s. The ultimate slowing of technological innovation had little to do with manmade rules governing equipment and more to do with Mother Nature herself. During the period that saw the greatest rate of technological advances, the author was intimately involved in the process of making the rules and trying (sometimes successfully) to simplify them.

Much of this writing is based on my personal knowledge and experience, augmented by historical research. I spent twenty-six years – from 1974 to 2000 – monitoring, formulating, and implementing the rules related to equipment. During this period, most of the significant technological changes in equipment were made and many innovations of some significance were introduced. Once advanced technology and good science were introduced into the club- and ball-design process, we had to develop technically sound test procedures and conduct research to better understand how equipment worked. The rationale for the adoption of new rules may have been questionable, but the process was transparent to everybody and the rules were, in most cases, unambiguous and relatively easy to implement.

**This is not so today**, and there is a trend to introduce rules and limits without ample justification and for questionable reasons. It is appropriate to use science to better understand how equipment works and what its potential is, but drawing up specifications that would impress NASA is uncalled for in golf – especially when there is no sound evidence that a problem exists.

I believe the rules makers have swung too far and now have a somewhat lopsided view of what the rules should protect, and I fear that the resulting changes are largely a way for the ruling bodies to demonstrate relevance. The USGA does not have to do this; it is the governing body and should build respect rather than barriers between itself and its constituents. To do this most effectively it must be transparent about its deliberations and justify the changes contemplated.

The object of this book is to provide a written document of how, why, and when equipment has been regulated and to consider the effect of these regulations. Has the game benefitted, and is it healthier because of the changes? This is a question that must be answered, and should be pondered long before any rule is written.

It is important to believe that the guardians of the game have control of the reins and will not let anything detrimentally affect the game, also that they will use sound technology and good science to cope with the onslaught of products and innovations brought on by commercially driven forces. The USGA holds its authority to govern the game through the consent of the governed. To its constituents it must be open and forthright for it to remain a respected body. Transparency is the key to loyalty.

I believe common sense and reason will ultimately prevail. There is too much good in the game of golf for it not to.

CHAPTER ONE

## In the Beginning

The Rules of Golf waste no time before acknowledging the central role of equipment in the game. Right there in Rule 1-1, it says, "The Game of Golf consists of playing a *ball* with a *club* from the *teeing ground* into the *hole* by a *stroke* or successive *strokes* in accordance with the Rules."

Several of those words are in italics in the original, to show that they can be found in the Definitions section of the Rules. "Teeing ground," "stroke," and "hole" are all defined there; "ball" and "club" are not. Why should they need to be? Everyone knows what a club and a ball are.

The earliest known code of golf rules, the 1744 regulations of the Honourable Company of Edinburgh Golfers (then known as the Gentlemen Golfers of Leith), refers frequently to clubs and balls: "You must tee your ball within a club's length of the hole.... You are not to change the ball which you strike off the tee.... No man at holling [sic] his ball is to be allowed to mark his way to the hole with his club or anything else.... If you draw your club in order to strike and proceed so far in the stroke as to be bringing down your club, if then your club should break in any way, it is to be accounted a stroke." One reference is unusually specific: "Neither trench, ditch, or dyke made for the preservation of the links, nor the Scholars' Holes or the soldiers' lines shall be accounted a hazard but the ball is to be taken out, teed and play'd with any iron club." This rule defines areas we would now call "ground under repair" and dictates that an iron club must be used after taking relief. (Irons were used for short shots and recoveries in the days when the ball was stuffed with feathers; wood clubs that swept at the ball were far more effective at hitting featheries for distance.)

As the game was played locally, for recreation, there was no need for a central authority to issue rules and regulations. Groups of players formed clubs for the same reason many do today: to gather a like-minded set of companions for friendly competitions and spirited repasts (some extremely spirited). According to Kenneth G. Chapman's thorough history, *The Rules of the Green*, "Many early Scottish golfers were also Freemasons. It seems that golf served primarily to whet their appetites for the gluttonous feasts laced with the liberal amounts of drink so important to their meetings. For them the main purpose of the game was what we know today as the nineteenth hole – as it is for many modern players as well."

The rules of the game could vary significantly from one location to another, depending on the traditions and conditions encountered at each. There were as many as thirty different codes adopted by various clubs between 1750 and 1850, most following the Honourable Company's model. By the second half of the nineteenth century, however, the Royal and Ancient Golf Club of St. Andrews (R & A) saw its influence increase, thanks to the spread of the British railway system and the opening of the St Andrews Railway in 1852. When Prestwick Golf Club was founded in 1851, it chose to follow St. Andrews's rules, no doubt influenced by its Keeper of the Green, Tom Morris. Prestwick hosted the first dozen Open Championships, played under rules all but identical to those of the Royal and Ancient.

Once the Open had become an annual event, there was a growing consensus that rule-making authority should be held by one body alone. Arguments broke out over which clubs should be represented on such a committee, and only the R&A was recognized as being above the fray. In 1897, with the explicit sanction of the other existing clubs, the R&A created a Rules of Golf Committee to issue a set of rules and to make decisions on matters of interpretation when asked to by the secretary of a golf club or association. The committee would be permitted to propose changes to the Rules, but such changes would have to be ratified by a two-thirds vote of the R&A's members at a general meeting.

In the first full set of rules issued and approved in 1898, the only one concerning the details of equipment describes what to do when a ball is damaged in the course of play:

> If a ball split into separate pieces, another ball may
> be put down where the largest portion lies, or if two
> pieces are apparently of equal size, it may be put
> where either piece lies, at the option of the player.
> If a ball crack, or become unfit for play, the player
> may change it on intimating to his opponent his
> intention to do so. Mud adhering to a ball shall not
> be considered as making it unfit for play.

Balls that broke in pieces were a problem for the gutta perchas, solid spheres of tree resin molded into playing shape. If a guttie broke, you could take the bits, boil them up, and make a new ball. The gutta percha's day would come to an end soon, as would any chance that the ruling bodies could avoid making decisions about equipment.

Around the time this formal set of rules was being established, a Cleveland industrialist named Coburn Haskell had a brainstorm. He was visiting a friend at the B.F. Goodrich plant in Akron, and while waiting he picked up some loose threads, wound them idly together, and bounced the resulting mass off the floor. It occurred to him that this would make for a lively golf ball, maybe add some yards to his drives. He suggested to his friend, a company manager named Bert Work, that they try to design a prototype.

Their early efforts were hard to control, but they eventually settled on a solid inner core for stability, stretched rubber windings around it for resiliency, and a cover to hold the thing together. The Haskell ball was patented in 1898, and it was the Pro V1 of its day, taking the golf world by storm.

Early reports suggested that the wound ball went twenty to fifty yards farther than the gutta percha. It was certainly more forgiving on mishits; you had to strike a guttie very precisely to get a good flight out of it. The wound ball required practice to adjust to its lively bounce in the short game, but within five years of its introduction the Haskell ball had almost completely replaced its solid predecessor, and it held its place in the golf world for nearly the entire twentieth century.

Traditionalists raised an alarm that will be familiar to anyone following equipment arguments today. The game will become too easy! The great old courses will be ruined, made obsolete! Interestingly, the complaint (as reflected in a poll taken by *Golf Illustrated*) was that the ball gave too much benefit to short hitters with good short games; long hitters would lose their rightful advantage. John L. Low, a great international amateur golfer, prolific writer, and longtime chairman of the R&A Rules Committee, believed the ball threatened the purity of the game and called for the establishment of a standardized golf ball.

The Rules Committee took up the issue, passing a motion in September 1902 stating "(t)hat the new rubber-filled balls are calculated to spoil the game of golf as now played over links laid out for the gutty ball and that it would be advisable to bring in a new rule for the regulation of balls and clubs to be used in playing the game." Low, who seconded the motion, believed this was a vote for full standardization; it proved not to be, though it was the first step onto the slippery slope of regulation that confronts us today.

Horace Hutchinson wrote a letter to *Golf Illustrated* against standardization that raised an important point: "The best merit of the Haskell ball and the reason it will prevail is that it makes the game much more pleasant to play because it leaves the club so easily. After all, we do pretend and assume that we play the game for pleasure." The two-time winner of the British Amateur had the good sense to look at the question in terms of what was best for all golfers, rather than being overly concerned about the effect on championship play. (For this, and many other excerpts from the historical record, I am deeply grateful to John Behrend, Peter N. Lewis, and Keith Mackie for their invaluable history, *Champions and Guardians: The Royal & Ancient Golf Club 1884-1939*, published by the R&A.)

The professionals were generally opposed to the new ball, and their association asked the R&A to mandate the use of gutties at the Open Championship. The pros were not disinterested observers: A lot of their income came from making and repairing clubs and balls. The guttie was simple enough to fashion (or remake after it broke) that a pro could do it in his shop; this was not true for a wound ball. Also, the resilient Haskell ball was easier on wooden club heads than the solid gutta percha, resulting in fewer broken clubs and thus fewer repairs. Despite the PGA's official position, one of its founders, J.H. Taylor, switched to the Haskell ball in competition.

In the spring of 1903, the R&A's Rules Committee met to vote on the proposed rule that had been drafted as a result of the motion back in September. It was defeated by a 10-5 vote. A month later, the top five finishers in the Open Championship all used Haskell balls. Resistance was futile.

This early battle over the "bounding billy" reflects many of the strains that would characterize equipment regulations in the century to come. An eloquent faction could be counted on to oppose any change in the status quo, waving the banner in support of the shot values of the great old courses (so much younger in those days). There would be an ongoing need to balance the pleasure of the players with the challenge of sport: At what point does a new technology make the game too easy? Perhaps the truest statement was the one made in a *Golf Illustrated* editorial: "I feel certain that no power on earth, except perhaps the police, will deter men from using a ball that will add to the length of their drive." The R&A was not yet ready to give itself that policing authority, but the day would come soon.

There is an oft-told story about the first specific insertion into the Rules of Golf of a direct prohibition of a type of club. It began with the unthinkable: an Australian-born American named Walter Travis winning the British Amateur championship in 1904. Travis defeated a much longer hitter by showing an especially deft touch on the greens, wielding a putter made by Arthur Knight of Schenectady, New York. The shaft of this club, soon referred to as the "Schnectady putter," connected to the center of the club's head rather than the more traditional heel. The British golfing establishment did not take kindly to being defeated by a foreigner – an American, no less – and focused its ire not on the individual but on his magic wand. Evidently, the center-shafted putter made the game too easy, so the rules-makers moved swiftly to banish it from the sport so that the skill and craft that led to championships would be that of the golfer, not the manufacturer. The United States Golf Association, while generally coordinating its rules with those of the R&A, recognized the insult inherent in this regulation, and so it never adopted this British rule.

It's a fine story, with the requisite measure of British disdain and American cheek, but there are a few holes in it.

To begin with, Travis won his title in 1904, but according to *Champions and Guardians*, there is nothing in the R&A's minutes to suggest any ruling on any club design was contemplated until 1907. That ruling involved a putter that was banned because it was "a mechanical invention," not because of a specific configuration. The R&A's 1908 edition of the Rules, adopted that September and accepted by the USGA as of February 1909, included for the first time a section – not within the numbered Rules themselves – called "Form and Make of Golf Clubs." That section read, in its entirety:

> The Rules of Golf committee intimates that it will not sanction any substantial departure from the traditional and accepted form and make of golf clubs, which, in its opinion, consist of a plain shaft and a head which does not contain any mechanical contrivances, such as springs.

No mention of a center shaft, no evident axe to grind against Travis and his ilk; the committee is concerned that some brilliant inventor will devise a club that works as a hitting machine or one that boosts distance by putting a literal trampoline onto or behind the face. Never mind that a spring would be ineffective; no coil could compress and recover in the brief time a ball is in contact with the clubface. They didn't know that then, and most likely they couldn't have known it, having no way of measuring the full forces of impact or its intervals of time. Nonetheless, the Rules of Golf Committee of the R&A had taken the significant step of declaring its authority over what is an acceptable club design.

Around this time, a gentleman named F.W. Brewster wrote a letter to *Golf Illustrated*. Brewster was the inventor of Simplex clubs, a design in which the head is a cylinder with the hitting face at its end, flattened at an angle to provide loft. For obvious reasons, the clubs were also referred to as "torpedo clubs." Brewster noted the vagueness of the clause and zeroed in on the difficulty of determining where and when "tradition" begins, and thus what constitutes a departure.

Almost a year later, a club in New Zealand wrote to the R&A to ask whether a small croquet mallet could be used as a putter. The Rules Committee's response was that "a croquet mallet is not a golf club and is inadmissible." You can almost see the flared nostrils and upturned lips as they deliver that response. Tautology, anyone? A croquet mallet cannot be used as a golf club because it is a croquet mallet and not a golf club. Thanks; got it now.

Debate raged in the pages of *Golf Illustrated* about whether any golfing angels could dance on the head of this mallet-shaped pin. An editorial observed that this answer points up the need for the committee to give a clearer definition of what is and is not a golf club, "and we do not envy them the task." Bernard Darwin was quoted in the magazine, presumably making reference to clubs like the cylindrical Simplex: "A croquet mallet is not a golf club; does that mean that a golf club made on the lines of a croquet mallet is not a golf club?... [Such a club] is not a croquet mallet; at least nobody out of a lunatic asylum would attempt to play croquet with it. Does it or does it not come within the statement that a croquet mallet is inadmissible?"

In its efforts to codify the distinction between croquet mallet and golf club, the Committee chose to focus on the centered shaft and stuck to its decision with hidebound certainty. They may have feared that any deviation from a strict ban would open the door for all manner of unsightly evasions unless the rule were drafted with exquisite deftness. Better to ban 'em all – croquet mallets, torpedo clubs, Schenectady putters – and put a few innocent clubs in jail rather than let any guilty ones go free. *Golf Illustrated* editorialized that "(t)he Rules committee might have been better advised to allow these mallet-headed and centre-shafted clubs to die a natural death and reserve their energies to suppress any invention, either in club or ball, whether by mechanical devices or otherwise, that would make the game easier."

In May 1910 – six years after Travis's victory, which puts the lie to the notion of swift retribution – the general meeting of the R&A gave the Rules Committee the authority to amend the Form and Make clause to "declare that all clubs of the mallet type are a substantial departure from the traditional and accepted form and make of golf clubs." *Golf Illustrated* reported in June that the USGA had decided not to accept the R&A's resolution – even though there was no such proposal for a new rule yet, just an authorization. The USGA saw no reason to ban the Schenectady putter along with the other offending mallets and suggested defining a mallet as a club whose measurements are greater from the face to the back of the head than the width across the striking face.

At last, in September 1910, the R&A passed an addition to the Form and Make clause that read as follows:

> The Committee regards as illegal the use of such
> clubs as those of the mallet-headed type or such

clubs as have the neck so bent as to produce a similar effect. The Committee intimates that the following general consideration will guide it in determining whether or not a club is made in accordance with the above rule:

1. The head of a golf club shall be so constructed that the length of the head from the back of the heel to the toe shall be greater than the breadth from the face to the back of the head.

2. The shaft shall be fixed to the heel, or to a neck, socket, or hose which terminates at the heel.

3. The lower part of the shaft shall, if produced, meet the heel of the club or a point opposite the heel either to right or left when the club is soled in the ordinary position for play.

The USGA broke with the R&A and refused to add this provision. Instead, it altered the Form and Make to make its divergence clear (new wording in italics):

> *The United States Golf Association* intimates that it will not sanction any substantial departure from the traditional and accepted form and make of golf clubs, which, in its opinion, consist of a plain shaft and a head which does not contain any mechanical contrivances, such as springs: *it also regards as illegal the use of such clubs as those of the mallet-headed type, or such clubs as have the neck so bent as to produce a similar effect.*
>
> *The shaft of a putter may be fixed at the heel or at any other point in the head.*

*The term mallet-headed, as used above, when applied to putters does not embrace putters of the so-called Schenectady type. U.S.G.A.*

The Rules were thus amended to address explicitly the legality of a particular family of club. And the USGA and the R&A were in conflict about what to do and how to do it. This may have been the first time, but it would not be the last.

Consider the following two quotes:

"Our longest holes are little more than a drive and a putt. My feeling is that if the game continues to improve in the matter of its length and we get just a little more resiliency in the ball and a little better clubs than we have now, the game in [the] future will be relegated to the only place where it can be played, and that is on the great prairies of our Western country."

"If the carrying power of the ball is to be still further increased, all our golf courses will be irretrievably ruined as a test of the game."

These very modern sentiments were actually expressed in 1902 by USGA President R.H. Robertson and in 1910 by *Golf Illustrated*, respectively. The battle between rules makers and distance in golf has been going on for as long as there have been rules makers.

Much as the R&A had a decade earlier, the USGA took up the idea of a standardized golf ball at its annual meeting in 1912. A year later, the Executive Committee reported that it had conferred with the R&A, who told them they'd abandoned their own efforts because it was simply too difficult to come up with a satisfactory definition. "It was decided," the Executive Committee noted, "that it was both impracticable and impossible to prescribe a standard ball which should be free from objection, and which, if adopted, would in any way enhance the pleasure of the players or the best interest of the game." It is heartening to see enjoyment cited as one of the two guiding principles for the decision.

Still, being regulators, the USGA and R&A continued to fret over technology's advances and felt the need to do something about them. At the R&A's general meeting in 1920, the Rules Committee reported that "the USGA were in agreement with our general proposition that players and not the inventors should guide the development of the game." A delegation from the USGA met for the first time with its British counterparts that year, and both sides agreed to add a rule governing the size and weight of the golf ball – these being the two primary aspects that could be measured at the time. The following was added to the Rules on both sides of the Atlantic:

### The Limitation of Ball

The weight of the ball shall be not greater than 1.62 ounces avoirdupois and the size not less than 1.62 inches in diameter. The Rules of Golf Committee and the Executive Committee of the United States Golf Association will take whatever steps they think necessary to limit the power of the ball with regard to distance, should any ball of greater power be introduced.

Thus began an extended and futile effort to control the playing characteristics of the golf ball by tinkering with its physical dimensions. This was undertaken by the newly created Implements and Ball Committee (I&B) of the USGA, with the input and cooperation of the major equipment manufacturers. In its 1923 report, the I&B Committee observed that "the 1.62 golf ball has proved probably as satisfactory as any ball that could be adopted. Courses are laid out with regard to this ball and shortening the drive would necessitate a great many holes being re-arranged which would be deplorable."

Despite this apparent satisfaction, the committee and its R&A equivalent continued to try out other combinations. Tests with some 300 players were conducted at St. Andrews, Hoylake, Sandwich, Sunningdale, Muirfield, Deal, and Walton Heath. They discovered that controlling size alone was useless, and that golfers at all skill levels enjoyed playing a lighter ball relative to its size rather than a heavier one, within limits. The R&A had asked Dunlop to make balls that were 1.66 inches in diameter and weighed 1.41 ounces, and also ones at 1.62 inches/1.31 ounces. Most players preferred the heavier and larger combination of those two.

An R&A report in September 1924 evaluated a 1.66 inch/1.51 ounce ball and declared it was harder to control in crosswinds, "thereby favoring skill players rather than power players." The USGA was experimenting along the same lines, and believed a larger/lighter ball would allow for a greater variety of shots. The R&A hoped that would be true but was much more concerned about the wind effects, reflecting the differences between the links courses in Great Britain and the more sheltered environs in the U.S.

By 1926, the USGA decided the best configuration involved a diameter of not less than 1.68 inches and weight of no more than 1.55 ounces. It proposed these specifications to the R&A, which responded without enthusiasm, arguing that the ball wouldn't do enough to limit distance to make it worth the hassle for manufacturers. The R&A stayed with the 1.62/1.62 ball; the USGA switched to the 1.68/1.55 specs effective January 1, 1931. The I&B Committee reported in early 1931:

> The new standard 1.68 x 1.55 ball has been a subject of major interest, and had been used in play far more extensively than published accounts would indicate.... The average golfer has discovered he can make shots with the new ball that were beyond his control with the old. He has found little or no loss of distance – he is continually playing from better lies, and he is amazed to find his scores averaging lower. This is also the case with women golfers who are playing noticeably better golf with the new ball. In a recent driving contest a well-known professional using the new ball won with an average 256 yards against the wind for three drives, while the other competitors used the 1.62 ball.

Once it was put into widespread play, however, reaction from the average golfer was swift and vehement. Charles McD. Puckette, writing in *The New York Times Magazine*, observed wryly that "about the new 1.55-1.68 golf ball – which won't even hit the green when accurately played, or stay in the hole on a perfectly straight putt – views are clear and fluent.... If [the] remarks concerning the authorities who prescribed this golfer's pill were directed against any branch of the government he could be arrested under the criminal syndicalism law for incitement to violence and riot." By July, USGA President H.H. Ramsay told the paper, "We are just sitting back and taking it on the chin for the time being."

Handicap players believed they were losing a little bit of distance and that the new ball exaggerated their hooks and slices. Professionals didn't see much difference, though they did feel the new ball didn't putt as well on fast greens. With time, they most likely would have adjusted their touch to reflect the lighter ball, but the outcry from the public was too great to ignore. As William D. Richardson wrote in the *Times*, "Distance-getting, however, has become a fetish with golfers, and those who find themselves thus curtailed are naturally concerned about it and it so happens that they are the ones who are most apt to give vent to their displeasure."

The USGA responded with unusual swiftness. In November, it announced that it would keep the increased size, but raise the weight maximum back to 1.62 ounces. The I&B Committee analyzed the debacle in its report for the year:

> The first balls on the market were over-size and substantially under weight, which combined with the generally unfavorable weather, brought a storm of protest. About June, with the specifications more nearly approached and the weather normal, a marked difference in attitude toward the ball was expressed, and more accurate and valuable information on its performance was obtainable. By September, it was clearly evident that the size of the ball was uniformly popular and preferable to play, by the average golfer, to the 1.62 size. The complaints of the ball narrowed down to two, namely, that there was insufficient weight to hold its course or bore into adverse winds, and that on the putting green it was too easily diverted by irregularities of surface as its power was spent. During the playing season extensive tests were conducted with balls of increased weight in the 1.68 size, and in November a ball of not less than 1.68 inches in diameter and not more than 1.62 ounces avoirdupois was adopted to become effective for play January 1, 1932.... Your Committee is of the opinion that a ball of this specification combines the most desirable features of any ball produced, and that it will prove eminently satisfactory in the hands of golfers at large.

The Committee was correct in this prediction, as the 1.68/1.62 ball is the one in universal use today. Even the R&A eventually converted to it – nearly sixty years later. (The 1.68-inch limit was adopted for all R&A championships in 1983, and the Rules change was announced in the 1988 code, effective January 1, 1990.)

The issue of ball size was always a stalking horse for a discussion of distance. In 1926, William C. Fownes, Jr., a former U.S. Amateur champion and son of the founder and designer of Oakmont, was head of the USGA's I&B committee, and in his annual report he wrote:

> The Committee is strongly of the opinion that
> a standard ball should be adopted just as soon
> as possible. As the matter stands today, the
> manufacturers are continually competing among
> themselves to produce balls of longer driving power,
> and in the absence of restrictive legislation they
> must do this in self defense. As a consequence,
> courses must be continually lengthened to meet this
> condition, and when this is done the balance between
> the ball and the course will be restored, but at the
> expense of a constantly increasing cost for upkeep.

A year later, Fownes was USGA President. He continued to call for standardization of the ball, arguing that "[p]erhaps one of the greatest services which we can render to the game is to fix and determine the most important implement of the game, which is the ball." He recognized the futility of controlling distance by tinkering with size and weight alone, since testing had shown that to reduce driving power would require a ball so large and light that it would greatly diminish the pleasure of the game. (This is exactly what the USGA discovered four years later when it did dictate a larger, lighter ball, during Ramsay's presidency.) Fownes recognized that the important issue was the ball's resilience, and set about trying to find a way to measure this vital quality.

At Fownes's urging, the I&B Committee worked extensively with Professor Harold A. Thomas of the Carnegie Institute of Technology in Pittsburgh to design a machine that could test resilience in a repeatable and reliable way. Fownes displayed the machine at the USGA's annual meeting at the Pittsburgh Athletic Club on January 8, 1927. A cylinder equal in weight to the head of a driver was shot upward through a brass pipe that had a golf ball resting on top of it. The speed of this striking cylinder would be set at 130 feet per second, corresponding to the driver speed of a first-rate golfer (perhaps true in hickory days – the speed equals 88.6 miles per hour). The ball was propelled upwards at a speed of about 220 feet per second (150 mph, a ball speed more expected from a 105 mph swing today), and was caught in a tapering metal tube sliding freely between vertical guides; a brake was applied to the striking cylinder to keep it from following the ball into the tube. By considering the weight of the riser and the height of its rise, the velocity of the ball would be determined; comparison of this velocity with the known velocity of the cylinder would provide the ball's "coefficient of resilience."

All very scientific, and if the thing had worked and the USGA had had the nerve, we might not have so much talk about the golf ball these days. Unfortunately, despite Fownes's evident passion for the project – he paid to have eight such machines created and one sent to the R&A – the device did not live up to expectations. The original design had to be tweaked to eliminate such variables as air pressure and friction and to reduce the need for a skilled operator. Further testing ensued, casting doubt on the accuracy and repeatability of its findings. More critically, the ball manufacturers were opposed to creating a resilience standard, fearing they would no longer be able to advertise balls on the basis of their comparative length. Herbert Jaques, Jr., chairman of the I&B committee, noted resignedly in his 1930 report, "We have had meetings with the Association of Golf Ball Manufacturers and ultimately it was decided inadvisable to include at this time a specification covering resilience...the new standard [1.68/1.55] ball is slightly more resilient than the present ball, and no attempt has been made to reduce its power through resilience control."

Any immediate concerns about the liveliness of the ball were pushed aside by the uproar over the introduction of the "balloon ball" and its subsequent decommissioning. The USGA may have felt some sympathy for the manufacturers, who'd had to alter their machinery twice in a year. Nonetheless, by the mid 1930s, the doom-criers were back in full throat. At the U.S. Open at Baltusrol in 1936, the USGA met with representatives of the major golf ball manufacturers and declared, according to the I&B committee report, "that the USGA viewed with alarm the increasing flight of balls during the past few years. Each manufacturer promised that he would not bring out for merchandising a ball of greater distance than those already on the market without first notifying us in writing. In addition, they said they would forward copies of their flight tests as they were made. The Implements and Ball Committee feels that the Association should do everything possible to discourage the increasing distance of the flight and roll of balls, and they are prepared to take whatever steps are necessary to see that this is done."

The R&A had similar worries. Its Rules of Golf committee sent a letter to its constituent golfing organizations in November 1938, asking if they would support specifications to reduce the distance the ball travels. "For the average long hitter," it read, "except under winter conditions, the three-shot hole practically does not exist. Old features of geographical and historical interest are now ceasing to affect the play of many famous golf holes. Wooden club play through the green, except against a head wind, is becoming a lost art. There is now difficulty in designing a sufficient number of long holes in the round which can be reached in two shots but which also give an opportunity for strategic play on the part of the shorter player who cannot get up in two." The letter, as quoted in *Champions and Guardians*, further notes that creating new back tees to challenge the long hitters could entail "a walk of over 100 yards in the direction opposite to that in which it is intended to play, [and] may add well over 1,000 yards to courses already stretched to 7,000 yards." (Is there a word in this that would be written differently today, with the possible exception of "wooden," which would now be called a wood but made of metal?)

The response to this letter was mixed. The European Golf Association was against reducing distance; New Zealand supported the R&A. The golfing unions of Great Britain and Ireland walked a tightrope, indicating they were against any increase in distance but not supporting a rollback. The Royal Canadian Golf Association (RCGA) also saw no problem with the present ball and did not feel its courses were endangered by it or future developments. It made a point in its reply that is as cogent today as it was then: "We believe that change in specifications in order to offset the power of a few championship players would meet with strong disapproval by at least ninety-five percent of those who support and make golf possible." The RCGA recognized that the problem under discussion only pertained to a tiny fraction of those who play the game.

The USGA continued to consult with the ball makers to develop some kind of test that would keep the ball in its present state forever. The prime motivation seems to have been fear of the unknown. A.M. Reid, USGA president in 1940, unknowingly admitted as much in his address to the association's annual meeting:

> We have been working, and the Association has spent quite a little money during this year, and will continue, until it is finished, in trying to construct a machine to measure the performance of a golf ball. We are convinced that any specifications to try to control the ball would be of value. We have no idea of cutting down the performance of the present ball in any way, but we feel that there is danger of somebody in the future discovering something which will make the golf ball go *a half mile, or something like that.* This machine, however, which the Armour Institute [of Technology, in Chicago] is building for us (as I say, at quite some expense) we think and hope is going to accomplish this for us. [Emphasis added.]
>
> This machine will merely, at great speed (it will be practical for the manufacturers), measure the efficiency of the ball: in other words, how far it will go on a given shot; and will merely eliminate the balls that will go over a certain distance.
>
> In other words, we don't care if they are under the distance or not; that is up to the manufacturer. But if the ball will, with a given blow, travel further than a specified distance, which we will try to figure out from the performance of the present-day good ball, why, then, it will be eliminated.

> We are in hopes that we are going to be successful
> with this machine. If we are not, it will be a big
> disappointment, because, as I say, we have spent
> quite a little money on it.

With the half-mile drive still barely a glimmer in John Daly's grandfather's eye, the USGA announced in 1941 that it had determined at last a standard to rein in potential distance gains. Effective January 1, 1942, encoded in the Rules of Golf alongside the size and weight limits, "The velocity of the ball shall be not greater than 250 feet per second when measured on the U.S.G.A.'s apparatus; the temperature of the ball when so tested shall be 75 degrees Fahrenheit; a maximum tolerance of 2% will be allowed on any ball in such velocity test." (This ball speed – 170.45 miles per hour – is still a good approximation of what a pro golfer can generate, not an exceptionally long hitter but an average Tour pro.)

Thus did the USGA begin its march to extreme specificity in regulating equipment. It is not enough to set a limit; it is necessary to specify the conditions under which the tests will take place, and to invoke a test tolerance to allow for the imprecision of machinery. I will have more to say about the inadvisability of such specifications in the next chapter.

The velocity standard had no immediate effect, as the manufacture of golf equipment was soon suspended for the duration of World War II. The test machine so lovingly created was dismantled and put into storage. It returned to action after the war, and though few balls were found to violate the velocity standard, the perception remained that distance was a clever and relentless enemy. Charles Peirson, new I&B chairman, reported in 1957 that "(t)he Implements and Ball

Committee has been concerned in recent years with the distance the modern ball can be struck. While existing testing methods give no conclusive proof that there has been any recent increase in distance, the history of the ball shows a long-term upward trend. Furthermore, over the last twenty or thirty years golf-course yardage has been increasing steadily.... It may be that a simple test of initial velocity is inadequate."

A new consultant was brought in; Arthur D. Little was given the task of examining the test procedures; a new driving machine was developed – but the velocity standard remained on the books and was supplemented by the Overall Distance Standard in 1976.

For several hundred years, while balls advanced from wood to feathers to gutta-percha to wound rubber, and clubheads went through a variety of shapes and sizes and woods and metals, one thing remained constant: the wooden shaft. Hickory, fashioned into a long dowel, connected the grip to the clubhead; it was strong enough to withstand the forces of the swing, yet had enough flex to provide a satisfying hitting action.

In the 1920s, club manufacturers started to experiment with steel shafts. They were easier to mass-produce than hickory shafts, and there was a greater supply; club makers were finding it increasingly difficult to obtain good wood. Pro shops began selling steel-shafted clubs alongside hickory, even though steel shafts were not approved by the USGA or the R&A.

The Executive Committee of the USGA took up the issue in 1922, deciding that the new material was "a distinct departure from the accepted form and make of golf clubs," and such clubs could not be used in USGA championships. In its 1923 report, the committee observed that "it does not appear that the steel shaft gives any greater distance to the long player; in fact, some tests have shown that the ball cannot be driven as far with the steel shaft as with the wooden shaft.... Tests made with the steel shaft against the ordinary hickory shaft seem to give greater length to a ball driven by a steel-shafted club while tests made with the best-selected hickory shafts give slight advantage to the wood." The committee emphasized that it had not reached a final decision, merely that it needed more testing and experience with the shafts before allowing it in championship play. (It is easy to forget that, even today, the USGA's jurisdiction extends only to its own events; all others who accept its rules do so by choice. It speaks well of the USGA's judgment in the past that nearly all golfers, professional and amateur, do so – though that is not always the case, as demonstrated by players who used steel clubs in the 1920s and those who used electronic distance-measuring devices in the 1990s and 2000s.)

In May 1923, in a meeting with the R&A rules committee, USGA President Frederick Byers indicated that the association probably would bar steel shafts. The following April, however, the I&B Committee wrote to the R&A, informing it that a decision had been reached and that it would now allow them. Its reasons:

> First: In the opinion of the committee the use of the steel shaft confers no playing advantages. Second: The use of steel shafts conserves the supply of hickory to an important extent. Third: The steel shaft is economical and of uniformly good quality, and can be profitably used by many players who now obtain only an inferior quality of hickory shafts.

This was a very sensible decision rendered for all the right reasons and with due caution. The USGA did not assume that steel shafts would replace hickory for everybody; Bobby Jones continued to use hickory shafts, and won the Grand Slam in 1930 with them. (The last major championship won with hickory was the 1936 U.S. Amateur, captured by John W. Fischer.) But the USGA recognized that mass-produced steel shafts could bring good-quality equipment to more people at a cheaper price, aiding the health of the game as a whole.

The R&A, naturally, did not go along, at least not at first. In May 1924, it formally expressed its displeasure that the USGA had gone ahead on its own, and it reaffirmed its own ban on the shafts. Several bodies asked the R&A for a local rule that would allow the use of steel. The first plea came from the Lima (Peru) Golf Club, with others from the Union des Golfs (France), the Australian Golf Union, and the RCGA (Canada). The Rules Committee in 1925 turned them down flat. The RCGA, cognizant of the large number of Americans competing in its tournaments, decided to allow the shafts anyway.

A year later, another plea came from Lima, saying that if players weren't able to use steel shafts, they'd have to wait months for new wooden ones. (Hickory shafts were prone to weakening with use; endless practice, as Ben Hogan and Vijay Singh know it, was not possible with the more fragile wooden shafts.) The R&A agreed to allow them under such exceptional conditions. The British Professional Golfers Association was opposed to steel shafts, fearing that club making would disappear as an art form with the rise of mass production; James Braid thought that would lead to a scarcity of professionals, since club makers and their assistants often moved on to become future pros. (By 1928, British PGA members were selling clubs with steel shafts, insisting that the demand was there and pros needed to hang onto their customers.)

In September 1929, the R&A Rules Committee noted that it had learned a great deal from its policy of allowing steel shafts in countries where it was hard to get good hickory, and they had clearly done no harm to the game. At its next meeting, the committee declared that steel shafts "conform with the requirements of the clause in the Rules of Golf on Form and Make of Golf Clubs" – acknowledging, in essence, that it couldn't enforce a ban despite its efforts over the past five years and that there was no reason to. Golfers wanted steel shafts; the R&A was losing prestige by trying to keep them from having them.

In stark contrast to this extended process, when I developed the graphite shaft for Shakespeare Sporting Goods and submitted it to the USGA in 1970 there was no debate, no concern, no reversals and no delays. In fact, there was never a formal approval process, or any ruling at all; no one said they didn't conform, and the lighter shafts were quickly adopted by golfers around the world.

The spirit of ingenuity in problem solving has always been a part of golf's appeal. This is as true for those who design and make clubs as it is for those who play them. We can see this in the evolution of the standard clubs, with heads becoming more streamlined, weight being centered behind the striking point for greater power, metal sole plates being added to wooden clubs to protect the head when playing from hard, rough surfaces like roads.

We can also see it the development of specialty clubs to deal with difficult situations. The small, round head of the rut iron is ideal to extract a ball from the channel left behind by a rolling wheel or a horseshoe print. Rake irons with their vertical teeth were designed to cut through water or mud or long grasses with less resistance than a solid-faced club (that was the theory, anyway). Dual-faced clubs increased the golfer's options; swan-necked irons offered a swerve where the hosel should be, making the club shank-proof (again, in theory).

Once they had chosen to take on the job of policing equipment, the governing bodies faced the task of defining which weapons were legitimate and which ran counter to the spirit of the game. As important, they had to determine and enumerate the principles that would guide their decisions.

We have already seen several stated repeatedly during the battles over the ball: Distance must be controlled to keep courses from having to grow exponentially. Balancing this concern is the belief that playing the game should give pleasure to the players. Another, which seems to have disappeared in recent decades, is that it is desirable to bring down the price of equipment to make golf more affordable for all, helping to spread and grow the game. This was stated explicitly at the USGA's annual meeting in 1922, when J. Frederick Byers declared, "We want to disillusionize [sic] the golfers of the country of the idea that golf is a rich man's game.... We have the assurance of Mr. [Julian] Curtis, President of A.G. Spalding & Company...that he is in absolute accord with [us] insofar as possible in the reduction of prices of golf equipment, and you have already seen the reduction in the price of the ball and the reduction in the price of the club." Curtis himself addressed the meeting, stating, "Seventy-five cents is the extreme price at which we are going to market a golf ball for some time to come. Anybody who is marketing a golf ball for any more than that price is taking advantage of the golfers of America."

A further essential principle is that a player's results should reflect his skill rather than the quality of his tools. This was spelled out by

H.H. Ramsay in his address at the 1930 USGA Annual Meeting:

> The new implements of the game, both in this
> country and abroad, bring problems to us almost
> daily. So long as the attempted improvements in
> golf clubs produce more durable clubs, or clubs
> which merely reflect improvement in manufacturing
> methods, the Association is not concerned. But
> when these new improvements depart substantially
> from the long-accepted form and make of the
> implements of the game, we are duty bound to
> act....
>
> In order that that there be no question with respect
> to the Association's policy in this regard, let me
> say that it is not the policy of the Association to
> encourage mechanical invention as applied to the
> implements of the game. What we do encourage
> is the development of skill with the ordinary
> acceptable implements.

Several innovations in the 1920s were found to be excessively ingenious and ran afoul of this principle. Jock Hutchinson, a born Saint Andrean who had become an American citizen, won the 1921 Open Championship at St. Andrews using a short-iron whose face had distinct raised ridges (like those on a cast-iron grill pan) to put extra spin on the ball. Such corrugated irons were permitted in America; the R&A considered them in February 1921, and recognized they did not violate the ban on mechanical contrivances. They were not a "traditional or accepted form," but unless the USGA agreed, the R&A Rules Committee did not want to appear to be purposely frustrating Americans coming over for the Open. In May, the committee declared that "grooved and slotted iron clubs (or any clubs which have the surface of the face fashioned in any manner in order to produce the same effect) do not conform…the use of them after 1ˢᵗ July 1921 shall be considered illegal." (The Open concluded on June 25.) The ruling also noted that clubs could be lightly scored or punched, as they had been for a long time.

British manufacturers insisted the ruling was too vague, and appealed for "a specific ruling as to the depth, width, and intensity of markings" that would be accepted. The R&A resisted giving an official definition of acceptable grooves – the issue can lead to all sorts of trouble, as I know well – leaving the matter in the USGA's hands. That body did not rule against these irons right away, even though USGA President Howard Whitney said of the corrugated irons, "It is self evident that they are destroying the science of the game of golf, and our Executive Committee is strictly opposed to their use." But in 1924, the following was added to the paragraphs on "Form and Make of Clubs" in the USGA rules:

> Club faces shall not bear any lines, dots, or other markings, made for the obvious purpose of putting a cut on the ball, nor shall they be stamped or cut with lines exceeding 1/16 inch in width, nor less than 3/32 inch apart, measured on their inside edges. Both line and dot markings may be used, either alone or in combination within the above limitations, provided all rough or raised edges are removed.

(Interestingly, in the 1928 rule book, the specific measurements were deleted, the first sentence ending after "cut on the ball," with "shallow" being inserted in the second sentence after "Both." The USGA on second thought may have agreed with the R&A about the inadvisability of providing a precise definition.)

When Ramsay of the USGA made the 1930 remarks quoted

above, he was referring to action taken to bar use of the "sandwedge" niblick. This was not the Sarazen sand wedge, unveiled in 1932, but a club patented by Edwin McClain in the U.S. and used by many, including Bobby Jones when he won the 1930 British Open. The club had a large, cambered sole (looking somewhat like the Alien Wedge) and a smooth, concave face. The concavity of the face – and those of irons that featured a face consisting of two angled pieces – made for an effective scoop in sand, but on shots from clean ground were likely to result in an almost imperceptible double-hit. Such clubs were banned by a new 1931 rule stating, "Club faces shall not embody any degree of concavity or more than one angle of loft." Club makers soon brought out straight-faced sand clubs, utilizing the bounce of the sole as in McClain's design but without the offending curve. The R&A had argued when first consulted that some degree of concavity should be permitted, but it went along with the USGA's total ban in 1934.

The biggest change in this era was the indirect result of allowing steel shafts. The best players soon recognized that the stiffness and uniformity of steel made it much more difficult for them to vary their shots through feel alone. Rather than having several swings and shot shapes for each club, golfers began to develop one swing they would use with every club. "Every club" could mean an almost limitless variety: Lawson Little, winner of the U.S. and British Amateur championships in 1934 and '35, was a long hitter with a deft short game, aided by the seven wedges he (or rather, his caddie) carried among his *twenty-six* clubs.

The USGA took note. In January 1936, the I&B Committee report stated, "For some time the Committee has noted with concern the increasing number of golf clubs carried by players. It is the opinion of the Committee that the carrying of so many clubs tends to minimize the skill of the game and make it too mechanical as well as increase the cost.... The Committee is not inclined to recommend at this time any change in the rules which would restrict the number of clubs the player might carry, but it earnest expresses the hope that the manufacturers and players alike will agree without thought that it is important to discourage the present tendency toward carrying such an excessive number of clubs."

Neither players nor manufacturers were in a rush to put themselves at what they considered a competitive disadvantage, and so the trend continued. In November 1936, Robert Harris, a former British Amateur champion and Walker Cup captain, proposed at an R&A Rules Committee meeting that players be restricted to a total of fourteen clubs. In his autobiography, *Sixty Years of Golf,* he derided the "twenty and even twenty-five clubs being carried by some players, in a quest for results which before were obtainable from five or six shafts of hickory." He dismissed those who kept adding clubs as trying to "buy the shot," and described how "knickerbockered, hobnailed, cloth-capped British sportsmen were inflicting unnecessary hardship and stunting the growth of the small boys and girls of France and Belgium by the weight of their golf bags."

His idea was accepted quickly, with both the R&A and USGA passing fourteen-club limits in 1938. The USGA's I&B committee's statement was explicit about its reasons:

> (T)he Executive Committee has noted with concern
> a growing increase in the number of clubs. Its
> inquiries supported its conclusion that limiting
> the number of clubs would tend to restore to the
> game individual shot-making skill lost through the

introduction of an excessive number of clubs in finely graduated and matched sets. The Committee felt that a multiplicity of clubs tended toward mechanization of a game one of whose great virtues lies in the opportunity it affords for full individual skill.... It was felt that, as a former President of the Association said, players should not buy their shots but should develop skill by their own effort.

The Executive Committee believes that limitations of the number of clubs will accomplish other desirable objections, namely:

1. Relief to caddies from unfair burdens;

2. Reduction of delays in play, as the players will spend less time in deciding what club to use;

3. Give players who cannot afford an unlimited supply of clubs an opportunity to compete with others on a more equal basis.

The importance of this rule was underscored by its inclusion in the preamble to the Rules of Golf, which now read, "The game of golf consists in a ball being played from the teeing ground into the hole by successive strokes, with clubs (not exceeding fourteen in number) and balls made in conformity with the directions laid down in the clause on 'Form and Make of Golf Clubs and Balls.'"

The fourteen-club rule was an almost perfect solution to a problem, protecting both the challenge of the game and its fairness in one simple, economical step. If the professional tours today are concerned about the best players making the game too easy, playing purely with power rather than displaying their shot-making skills, they could easily learn the lesson here and reduce the number of clubs allowed to each player. A ten- or even eight-club limit would force the pros to hit more varied shots with each chosen implement; it worked in the late '30s, and it would work in the twenty-first century as well.

One last change that followed from this limit was a ban on clubs with multiple faces. An iron with dual hitting surfaces – one loft in front, another to the rear – would allow the player to circumvent the fourteen-club rule. The one exception was for putters whose faces had substantially the same loft front and back; the Cash-In putter, a simple blade designed for Spalding in the 1930s by Robert Cash, is an example of a legal two-faced club that could be used by right- and left-handed golfers. The restriction joined the long-standing prohibitions of moving parts and adjustable elements in guiding decisions on individual clubs rendered by the I&B committee.

It would be an exaggeration to say that all the significant rules and regulations that would govern equipment were in place by the start of World War II, but only a slight exaggeration. In the postwar period, science took a large leap forward, and while the ball continued to resist standardization, the age of microspecification was dawning, and bigger and bigger decisions were to be made about smaller and smaller distinctions.

Before that could happen, there was one final major breakthrough of note: the joint revision of the *Rules of Golf* issued by the USGA and the R&A in 1951. Some differences between the two sets of rules were eliminated: The R&A accepted elimination of the stymie in match play and removed its restriction on center-shafted putters. One major difference remained: the size of the ball; the R&A clung to its 1.62-inch minimum. But the principles that held sway over equipment were shifted from the separate "Form and Make" section and the preamble into the body of the Rules itself. Here's how it read:

## RULE 2

### The Club and the Ball

1. **Legal Clubs and Balls**

   Players shall not use clubs or balls which do not conform to the regulations laid down in Clauses 2 and 3 of this Rule.

2. **Form and Make of Clubs**

   a. No golf club will be sanctioned that embodies any substantial departure from the traditional and accepted form and make.

   The golf club comprises a plain shaft and a head which do not contain any mechanical contrivances, such as springs.

   Insets in the faces of iron clubs are not allowed.

   Club faces shall not embody any degree of concavity on the hitting surface, and shall not bear any lines, dots, or other markings with sharp or rough edges made for the obvious purpose of putting additional spin on the ball. Markings on iron clubs shall conform with USGA specifications. (See Note to this Rule).

   b. The following general considerations will guide the USGA in interpreting the above:

   **Shape of Head**

   The head of a golf club shall be so constructed that its length from the back of the heel to the toe shall be greater than the breadth from the face to the back of the head.

   **Attachment of Shaft**

   The shaft shall be fixed to the clubhead at the heel. It

may be attached by means of a neck, socket, or hose which shall be so constructed that the shaft shall be in line with the heel or with a point opposite the heel, either to right or left, when the club is soled in the ordinary position for play. However, the shaft of a putter may be fixed at any point in the head.

### Nature of Grip

The grip shall be a continuation of the shaft to which material may be added for the purpose of obtaining a firmer hold. The grip shall be substantially straight and plain in form, may have flat sides, but may not have a channel or a furrow or be molded for any part of the hands.

### Movable Parts Prohibited

A club shall be one unit. All its various parts shall be permanently fixed. No part may be movable or separable or capable of adjustment by the player.

**NOTE:** *Players in doubt as to the legality of clubs are advised to consult the USGA. Specifications for markings on iron clubs have been issued to manufacturers.*

*If a manufacturer is in doubt as to the legality of a club which he proposed to manufacture, he should submit a sample to the USGA for a ruling, such sample to become the property of the USGA for reference purposes.*

3. **Weight, Size and Velocity of Ball**

The weight of the ball shall be *not greater* than 1.620 ounces avoirdupois, and the size *not less* than 1.680 inches in diameter.

The velocity of the ball shall be not greater than 250 feet per second when measured on the USGA's apparatus; the temperature of the ball when so tested shall be 75 degrees Fahrenheit; a maximum tolerance of 2% will be allowed on any ball in such velocity test.

4. **Exception**

   In international team competition the size of the ball shall be not less than 1.620 inches in diameter, and the velocity specification above shall not apply.

   **PENALTY FOR BREACH OF RULE:** *Disqualification*

   **NOTE:** *The Rules of the Royal and Ancient Golf Club of St. Andrews, Scotland, provide that the weight of the ball shall be not greater than 1.620 ounces avoirdupois, and the size not less than 1.620 inches in diameter.*

All was not so simple and plain – the separate section regarding Markings on Iron Clubs included three pages of specifications – but the necessary rules were now pretty much in place. The medieval game was ready to enter the space age.

CHAPTER TWO

# The Age of Science

When I joined the USGA in 1974, my first major assignment was to develop an Overall Distance Standard for golf balls and clubs. The motivation for this, as always, was fear – fear of potential distance gains from some unforeseeable innovation.

There was already an Initial Velocity (IV) standard, adopted in 1942 based on results using the Armour IV test machine, but it did not take into account the aerodynamic effects on a ball in flight. The Executive Committee in the 1950s had initially explored limits on ball compression – perhaps as a result of some locker room discussion – even though any compression effect would show up in the ball's initial velocity. No such regulation ever made it into the rules, but the conversation led to a more scientific examination of the forces that control the final results of club-to-ball contact.

In 1957, the Arthur D. Little Company was commissioned to make a comprehensive study of the flight of the ball. A launching machine was purchased in 1959 from the MacNeill Engineering Co. of Waltham, Mass. It was a dual striker machine that could test two balls at the same time. Balls were fed onto two separate hollow rubber tees just below the machine's striking zone; they were held in place by a partial vacuum and lifted into the strike position between rotations of the arms. The arms, about three feet long, rotated continuously and had a striker plate attached to the end of each. Plates could be attached with various angles of impact obliqueness to simulate the loft of different clubs. The machine was initially housed at Winged

Foot Golf Club and used to test balls outdoors.

In1963 the USGA engaged an independent testing agency, United States Testing Company, to check golf balls for weight, size and IV; the testing procedure had become more than the USGA's staff and committeemen could handle. Manufacturers were sending balls to the USGA for testing before putting them on the market. In order to create uniform conditions, the manufacturers asked for the ball size tests to be conducted at 75 degrees F. The USGA rejected this request at the time, since it would make field testing impractical: Officials on the first tee could only test a ball if the temperature that day was precisely 75 degrees. By 1971, the Initial Velocity ball tests were being conducted on both the Armour machine and a new machine developedby Illinois Tool Works (ITW). The ITW machine was designed to measure the Coefficient of Restitution (COR) of the ball when struck with a solid, heavy object – a rotating striker-and-wheel mechanism weighing approximately 250 pounds. This new machine was commissioned by the USGA in 1966 (completed in 1969), and the dual testing was supposed to determine how best to convert to the new and presumably more efficient ITW apparatus.

A year later, the I&B committee became even more "standards-conscious," believing there was a burgeoning need to control the ball and clubs and that precise standards were the way to go about it. A proposal was made to adopt a maximum Radius of Gyration standard (related to Moment of Inertia) for balls, which the committee believed would limit the spin that could be applied to the ball; and a shaft standard to control materials. An extensive study was conducted on the differences between the weight, flex, vibration frequency, and other properties of steel and aluminum shafts. The study did not address the relationship between these physical properties and their effect on launch conditions or any other performance factors. There was no technical basis for these studies – they were purely done to determine the different properties of the two shaft materials – but the committee believed the results would lead to a way to control equipment.

In 1972 the USGA acquired a mechanical golfer developed and built by the True Temper Company in the late 1960s for the purpose of testing shafts. The USGA bought it to test balls and clubs. The mechanical golfer's swing was based on photographic analysis of the swing profile – from the top of the backswing to impact – of Byron Nelson, Toney Penna, and others. This machine was initially given the nickname "Iron Mike," until Frank Hannigan objected: "Not Iron Mike," he said, "Iron Byron."

When I got a chance to evaluate the machine late in 1973 and again soon after I joined the USGA in 1974, I was satisfied that it was accurate enough to use in developing an overall distance standard (ODS) for golf balls. I had already concluded it would be impossible to devise a similar standard for clubs; a club is a system of parts, each of which contributes somewhat to distance, and the permutations of lengths, shafts, weights, heads, lofts, and so on would make it far too complicated to concoct a meaningful distance standard for clubs. I told Ken Gordon, then chairman of the I&B committee, that I believed setting an ODS for balls was possible and could be done within eighteen months or so, depending on the weather, but an ODS for clubs was not feasible using this machine without isolating the properties and effects on ball performance of the individual component parts.

The initial test hut was moved from a downward-sloping range in front of Golf House (USGA headquarters in Far Hills, NJ) to a newly graded, level driving test range 335 yards long.

The test consisted of driving balls onto the range under controlled launch conditions, taking the ambient conditions into account and adjusting for them. The launch conditions closely represented those of the best players for swing speed, launch angle, carry, and roll distance.

We recruited a local pro golfer, Mike Souchak, who was known for his ability to drive a long way and who was reasonably consistent. Using a club that was common on Tour, Mike spent days hitting balls while we took measurements of the head speed and launch conditions as well as the resulting distance. These measurements included time in flight, carry distance, roll, temperature, relative humidity, wind and barometric pressure, etc. We used Mike for these tests to establish and approximate the clubhead speed and other conditions typical of a long-hitting Tour professional at the time. Because we were trying to create a ball standard, not a golfer standard, we could have based our conditions on any consistent player, but we wanted the ultimate figure to relate to the objective: to limit the distance that the pros, who were making courses obsolete, could hit the ball. This would assure us that the distance standard was relevant and incorporated any advantage a long-hitting pro might have over golfers with lower head speeds.

With Mike as our starting point we experimented with a range of head speeds from 150 to 170 feet per second, and settled on 160 feet per second (108.8 mph). For a "standard test club" we used a Spalding laminated head with a 10 degree loft, D2 swing weight, stiff shaft, 44 inches in length. There were only a few adjustments we could make to the mechanical golfer to change the launch conditions, mostly variations of ball position and the approach path (to change launch angle). Shaft deflection just prior to impact based on shaft flex and acceleration rates of the swing also influenced launch angle and spin rate, but not significantly.

We hit a variety of balls: five wound balls that were used on Tour and two two-piece balls. The settings on the mechanical golfer were changed – holding the head speed constant – until we reached the maximum average distance for each of the balls. Once the settings were finalized, these were fixed, and we used the launch conditions of a solid ball – relatively stable in performance over time – to confirm that the test was properly calibrated every time it was conducted. The launch conditions for the calibration ball had to be exactly the same before and during every test. This was not a frivolous task, especially after the machine was repaired – it broke down frequently or the shaft broke after an undetermined number of hits. We eventually redesigned and built the basic structure of the machine (giving Iron Byron major surgery from the shoulders down), passing these design changes to the builders of the machine so they could modify all subsequent machines sold to the ball manufacturers.

There was some concern on the part of a few committee members who had heard about the "Critical Reynolds Number" (CRN) that the test speed was not high enough to take this phenomenon into account. The CRN is a point at which the drag forces through the air are suddenly reduced by as much as 50% on a nonspinning ball; the ball passing through this point gets an easier ride – a drag force barrier – until it slows down enough to slip out of the low drag-resistance condition and back into the higher drag forces experienced by slower balls. The committeemen wanted the swing speed and consequently the ball speed to be set sufficiently high to include this free or easier ride. In fact, the dimpled ball actually passes through this CRN barrier at less than 60 mph, and then only in a nonspinning mode. The CRN is a very localized phenomenon that complicates a clear understanding of airflow over a spinning ball, because the ball surface speed relative to the air is different over various parts of the ball due to its spin and its speed through the air. Obviously, spin affects this significantly. The dimple design also affects this very localized airflow going from laminar to turbulent flow – the separation point. The CRN is not a magical power-boost, as the committee members who were concerned about it believed.

One member of the I&B committee couldn't understand why we had to spend so much time calibrating and standardizing conditions and settings. He suggested that all we had to do was put the ball on the tee, push the fire button and "Let the f---ers fly." The technical staff adopted the acronym LTFF to describe some of the stranger ideas on how to conduct testing put forward by various committee members.

We had extensive meetings with the ball manufacturers as we were developing the ODS, and they were not very happy about any standard that would level their competitive field or affect their ability to promote and sell balls. "More distance" has been a crucial part of golf-ball marketing for nearly as long as there have been golf balls. The biggest companies felt that their advanced technology and production processes gave them an advantage that a limit would take away. In an attempt to get as much as they could, they argued for a 5% "innovative tolerance" that would allow them to introduce new products they already had in development on which they had spent a lot of money in the R&D process. We eventually agreed to a 4% innovative tolerance, on top of a 4% test tolerance – the manufacturers also wanted a 5% test tolerance. The test tolerance was precisely that, and we clearly stated that this would be reduced as test methods became more refined.

The standard was adopted in March 1976: "A brand of ball, when tested on apparatus approved by the USGA on the outdoor range at the USGA Headquarters under the conditions set forth in the Overall Distance Standard for golf balls on file with the USGA, shall not cover an average distance in carry and roll exceeding 280 yards, plus a tolerance of 8%. (Note: The 8% tolerance will be reduced to a minimum of 4% as test techniques are improved.)" We also included in a notice to manufacturers that if launch conditions – holding head speed (ball speed) constant – other than those established for the test were found to increase the distance balls would fly, the USGA would adopt these conditions for the test.

The 1976 adoption of the ODS didn't mean that a ball couldn't be driven more than 280 yards (302.4 yards when you factor in the tolerances); it meant that the ball could not travel farther than that, at the given swing speed and launch conditions. (The overall tolerance was reduced to 6% – 4% innovative tolerance and 2% test tolerance – in 1986.)

In the years that followed, engineers of all kinds became exponentially better at testing and modeling as a result of the computer revolution. Savvy manufacturers learned that they could design a ball that would meet the ODS under the test protocol, yet go farther under its own optimal launch conditions. The notice to manufacturers that we had included alongside the distance standard addressed this exact situation, so in the 1990s I proposed an Optimized ODS, in which no ball could exceed the specified distance *under its own optimal launch conditions*. This would have been a nightmare – an impossibility – if it required physical testing with trial-and-error hunt and peck experiments to determine those conditions, but computer modeling and aerodynamic measurements made in the Indoor Test Range ultimately allowed us to simulate optimum launch conditions.

The USGA never adopted an Optimized ODS. Manufacturers argued that they could hardly be held to a standard based on conditions that were different for every ball, and that unless those optimum conditions (spin and launch angle) were comparable to those on Tour, the result would be irrelevant. This tactic was frequently used by manufacturers to persuade the un-tech-savvy administrators to reject a limitation under consideration. The ODS is not a player standard, it's a ball standard; we were perfectly willing to increase the head speed for purposes of the test, but it would change nothing, since the expected distance would increase as well. The committee never clearly understood this, and the manufacturers were able to make the "relevance" argument with great success. (The manufacturers knew exactly what they were doing; at the same time they were arguing against an Optimized ODS, they were working with their professional players to help them achieve the optimum launch conditions for their balls.)

When the committee yielded on optimization, it gave up several more yards in the field compared to what the tests showed. In 2007, the USGA tweaked the ODS to reflect the increased swing speed of professional golfers, raising the clubhead speed for the test to 120 mph (176.2 feet per second) and using a titanium head with springlike effect to establish a new distance for the ODS. The distance was such that no ball on the list of conforming balls would fail; in other words nothing changed, but the numbers in the standard were now closer to the updated Tour reality, which seemed to comfort the guardians as it looked like something significant was being done. This was a feel-good thing for the committee, but it was not the best move and it was several years too late. The new distance standard jumped to 317 yards with a three-yard tolerance. This tolerance was an example of how advanced and effective the indoor simulation of overall distance truly was.

The announcement of the new standard was treated as though the USGA had caved in to the manufacturers by liberalizing its regulations, but in fact the two standards are virtually identical, the increased distance merely resulting from the faster swing speed and a different head construction. We should derive some comfort from this change, because it is moving slowly in the right direction, if only by baby steps. If the USGA continues to set the conditions close to those of Tour players, they'll wind up with an optimized standard by accident, because the Tour players are approaching and in most cases have arrived at their optimum launch conditions.

Still, the ODS is a pretty good standard, and it's based on the right kind of reasoning. It doesn't try to define a golf ball, set an exact limit on its resilience, dictate a particular dimple number or pattern, or specify permitted materials or composition. It doesn't concern itself with causes, just effects: Do whatever you want with the ball, but it can't go farther than X yards under these conditions. Adding the optimized element later would have closed whatever loopholes were left, but for its time it did what it was supposed to do, under conditions that represented the swing of a real golfer.

If you're as old as, say, Jack Nicklaus, you remember when computers were huge, unwieldy things that filled an entire room with mysterious cabinets that clanked and whirred (or at least that's what they did in the movies). The explosion of technology that I've seen in my lifetime was unimaginable outside the realm of science fiction. It speaks well of the beauties of golf that the game has survived and thrived through an age of such change and, yet, has done so in a form that would be readily recognizable to our ancestors.

That's not to say that golf is static or unchanging. There has been considerable change on the margins of the game, not merely in the principles and understanding of equipment, but in such diverse areas as agronomy, metallurgy, exercise physiology, and (alas) marketing. But for all the spectacular innovations in clubs and balls, it's probably still true that the most important technological innovation in golf in the twentieth century was the power mower. Small things have changed; the big picture remains pretty much the same. Golf could not have lasted for so many centuries if the basic fundamentals of the game were in constant flux.

The challenge for the ruling bodies in the last fifty years has been to incorporate the expanded knowledge reflected in high-tech equipment without overreacting to it. Microdesign does not have to lead to micromanagement. Club and ball designers were able to take scientific principles and apply them to what had mostly been an evolutionary trial-and-error process. It was inevitable that the regulators would respond in kind, examining the results in greater detail, perhaps in too much detail.

At the very beginning of this process, I&B chairman Clarence W. Benedict stated in his 1961 report that tests were being conducted to determine the effect of clubface roughness on backspin. "Surprisingly," he noted, "two independent and usually reliable sources have reported that club face roughness in the form of grooves and/or surface treatment has little or no effect upon backspin." The tests involved ultra-high-speed photography of balls painted with a heavy line around their circumference so the spin rate could be measured.

A year later, Benedict reported the upshot:

> The results of these tests were somewhat surprising, but tended partially to confirm the other reports that backspin did not depend upon clubface roughness. We found that when hit with the smooth-faced iron the ball attained a backspin of 62.5 to 261 RPS (revolutions per second). When struck with the rough-faced iron the backspin attained was from 206 to 250 RPS. This showed that, although it is possible to get as much backspin with a smooth-faced club as with a rough one, the average is much higher with the rough-faced one and the results much more consistent. In these tests the smooth-faced club gave an average of 166 RPS for all shots and the rough-faced club 224 RPS.
>
> Although it is apparently true that a smooth surface can produce equivalent or even greater backspin than a rough one in individual cases, the average backspin is much greater with the rough-faced club. For this reason, it would be impractical for the USGA to ease or eliminate the present regulations which control the markings on iron clubs.

(It needs to be noted that the test compared a smooth face with a grooved face. Subsequent tests have shown that a sand-blasted face gives more spin than a grooved face. The differences involved in the most recent groove change stem from groove shape and volume when a ball is struck from light rough; in really heavy rough, as at a U.S. Open, there is no distinction in performance among groove configurations.)

Those regulations adopted in 1942 already occupied four pages in the back of the rule book. In general – if such specificity can be called general – the specifications required that grooves be no wider than approximately 1/32 of an inch, that the angle between the flat surface of the clubface and the side of the groove must be at least 135 degrees, and the flat spaces between grooves must be at least three times the width of the groove. If the club had punch marks instead of grooves, those marks could not exceed "a slight amount over one-sixteenth of an inch in diameter."

Grooves would be a thorny issue in the decades to come, and the USGA would learn that no level of precision in the definition could eliminate the ability of manufacturers and lawyers to find (or argue) ambiguity.

At about this time, a General Electric engineer named Karsten Solheim decided to use his knowledge of physics to help lower his handicap. Solheim fell in love with golf as an adult, and he was entranced and bedeviled by it. He struggled with his putting, and he concluded that one major factor was the tendency of a putter head to twist upon making impact with the ball. To reduce that twisting, he came up with a design that moved weight away from the center of the face and towards the heel and toe. The original model supposedly consisted of two popsicle sticks connected to a pair of sugar cubes, one at either end. The metal face of the prototype version made a *ping* sound when struck on the sweet spot, and that became the name of the putter and the line of clubs he developed.

Solheim set up shop in Phoenix, then the site of the annual season-opening PGA Tour stop. He offered club-fitting services to the pros there and developed a reputation as a man who knew what he was doing with equipment. This helped him persuade the pros, one by one, to try out his new putter design. He knew it was based on good science and was confident it would catch on. He received a patent for his heel-toe weighted putter head in 1962, and that same year a Tour player named John Barnum became the first to win a PGA tournament using a Ping putter.

Karsten Solheim's breakthrough was based on his understanding of inertial properties and the value of increasing the Moment of Inertia (MOI). By spreading the weight away from the center of gravity and intended point of contact at the center of the clubface, he reduced the twisting that follows from off-center contact and sends a putt even farther off line than an imperfect stroke would by itself. If we all made perfect contact all the time, increasing the MOI wouldn't make a difference; since we don't, the change in weighting has the effect of increasing the size of the sweet spot and making the penalty for missing it less severe.

Four years later, Karsten Manufacturing Company brought out a more traditional-looking blade that still incorporated the weighting principles of his original two-plated design. This one, called the Anser, had a flange in the back with a cavity behind the center of the face. It was every bit as effective as the earlier model and went on to become the most successful putter ever, both in terms of sales and of tournaments won.

It took only a small step in logic to realize that if increasing the MOI was helpful in putting, it could be effective on full swings as well. The larger face of an iron would benefit from not merely moving weight to the heel and toe but all around its perimeter, top and bottom as well. A perimeter-weighted iron would be more forgiving, and because of the slight increase in distance involved in the imperfect shots, the improvement would be more obvious and more significant to the golfer.

Having made a brilliant theoretical breakthrough, Solheim now cemented his place in golf history with an equally important business decision. Heretofore, all irons were made through the forging process, as they had been since they were hand-hammered by smiths. Forged metal is hammered or stamped into shape while hot, resulting in thin, uniform blades. While it was theoretically possible to forge the kind of cavity-backed iron he had in mind, Solheim recognized it would be difficult and expensive. Instead, he turned to the investment casting process, a method that dates back to the time of the pharaohs.

In investment casting, a model of the head is carefully created out of brass or some other metal that's easy to carve or machine. This is then used to make a mold, which in turn is used to make wax replicas of the original machined model. This wax head is then dipped repeatedly in a ceramic slurry commonly made of plaster of paris mixed with a powdered silica to coat the head and build layers until there's a thick skin surrounding the wax model. This coated model is fired (baked) until it becomes very hard and the wax inside melts and vaporizes and comes out of a hole designed for this purpose. Molten metal can then be poured into the cavity through the hole, and it will take the shape of the original model. It's easier to create different shapes with this process than with the compression forces used in forging; it's also possible to use a wider variety of metals and alloys like stainless steel, which eliminates the need for further plating to prevent rust.

The original Ping Karsten I irons had a half-moon cavity in the back of the head. Golfers may not have understood why these clubs gave them better results than their old forged blades, but they flocked to perimeter-weighted clubs over the next twenty years. Ping brought out the wildly successful Ping Eye series; nearly all manufacturers followed suit, and investment casting took over the industry.

Karsten Solheim had the wisdom to design clubs that would help the average golfer. The pros didn't need the help; they make consistent contact on the sweet spot, and perimeter weighting makes it more difficult to work the ball the way the most skilled golfers like to through subtle variations in grip and technique. But handicap players benefitted, and the needs of the many created a marketing bonanza. In 1986 Bob Tway became the first player to win a major – the PGA – using investment cast clubs, Ping Eye2.

Investment casting saved money for all manufacturers as compared to forging. There was only one problem with it: It wasn't very good at making V-shaped grooves. This would have repercussions down the line.

I became intimately involved with the Rules of Golf in the early 1970s, after I joined the USGA. To a certain extent, the rules had been governed by common sense for a very long time. There were two primary objectives for the rules on equipment: the Challenge objective, and the Sameness objective.

The Challenge objective protects the difficulty of the game. We don't want golf to be too easy; we need it to be appropriately difficult so that it will test us, allow us to test ourselves. We acquire skill through study, practice, and repetition, so we may demonstrate it on the golf course and have it reflected in our scores, our handicaps, the thickness of our wallets after all the bets are paid. If a club or a ball takes away the challenge, if it makes the game too easy, then it takes away the reward we've earned in developing skill and gives the same results to anyone who can lay out the money.

The equipment rules ensure that our results are ours, not those of a clever inventor. The line is not always clear. Did the Sarazen sand wedge introduced in 1932 make the game too easy? Did concave-faced irons? Does perimeter weighting? The powers of golf ruled against the middle of these three and allowed the other two. Is there an obvious qualitative difference between the soldered flange that gave Sarazen's club bounce and McClain's earlier design? The R&A didn't think so, but the USGA argued persuasively that there was.

The Sameness objective guarantees us that the game we play will be similar to the game played by our great-grandfathers and will be again to our great-grandchildren. The "traditional and customary" clause is the prime guardian of Sameness. The principle also ensures that whatever individual choices we make within the spectrum of allowable equipment, we will all be playing the same game.

These guidelines were applied for many decades with a common understanding of the purpose of the game and the values that needed to be protected. As we entered the scientific age, we began to devise scientific solutions to the problems that arose. My charter was to help come up with those solutions. But the more I studied the questions, the more I realized that they were better off being treated with common sense instead of the kind of infinitesimal precision our technical expertise made possible.

Consider the case of the Polara ball. This was a golf ball designed with dimples around its equator but not at the poles. They may have thought that by eliminating the surface roughness from the sides of the ball when hit spinning about its pole axis, they would reduce the drag forces on the ball in flight, causing it to go farther. When hit with perfect backspin, the ball flew straight, though not as far as a standard ball. When hit imperfectly, with a sidespin component that normally causes a slice or hook, the ball would veer in the direction of the spin on its way up, then turn back in the other direction as it descended in a looping flight path. This self-correcting flight became the ball's promise, and the problem.

There was no rule specifically preventing a golfer from using a ball that corrects hooks and slices. But a true understanding of the purpose of the game makes it obvious that such a ball cannot be permitted. No rule dictates that a ball must have dimples over its entire surface, or a certain number of dimples, or dimples at all. We refused to place the ball on the conforming list, justifying the decision under the general rule banning "artificial devices that might assist him in making a stroke or in his play." (We couldn't use "traditional and customary" because in the rules at the time that clause appeared in the provisions governing clubs, not balls.)

In subsequent revisions, we added a Symmetry standard, stating that the ball "must not be designed, manufactured, or intentionally modified to have properties which differ from those of a spherically symmetrical ball." We originally added some well-defined specifications that included test procedures, but we later softened the limits and removed the test from the rule book itself, because the rule worked best when it governed *intent* rather than dictating specifics.

I increasingly have come to believe that intent is the essential factor in a well-drawn regulation. The Polara wasn't nonconforming because it failed to have dimples over some specific percentage of its surface; it was nonconforming because it was designed to perform differently from a symmetrical sphere.

Intent keeps you from getting lost in the trees when your

plan is to map the forest. It keeps your focus on the effect being achieved, rather than having to delineate and outlaw all possible improper means toward reaching an effect.

Take the rule that a shaft must be straight. Very few if any shafts are or can be made perfectly straight, so a specification would have to include a tolerance to allow for the practical problems inherent in all common manufacturing techniques. It would have to outline precisely the test method. Such specificity would allow a manufacturer with unique production capabilities to design a shaft that was deliberately crooked but was within the legal limits of tolerance. The manufacturer could declare that his shaft has successfully circumvented the USGA's efforts to keep superior technology out of your hands – whether it's superior or not – and the ruling body couldn't do a thing about it. Better for the rules to state that a shaft must be designed with the intent of being straight and to leave it at that.

Remember the great Dimple Race? Early in my term as Technical Director of the USGA, ball manufacturers staged a battle to put the most possible dimples on a golf ball. Marketers trumpeted the number as though it were a quality rating – if many are good, then more must be better. I've seen as many as 812 dimples on a ball and as few as 252. We never seriously considered adopting a rule governing the number of dimples, because it's unnecessary. The number is self-limiting to begin with: A ball with too many dimples will ultimately perform much like a smooth one – in other words, not as well as one with fewer dimples. It would be a nightmare to have to enforce such a rule, counting the dimples on every make and model of ball. But mostly, who needs the rule when there's already a limit on the ball's performance? The Overall Distance Standard governs the effects of all aspects of a ball's design – and an Optimized ODS would do so even better. Keep your eye on the effects and you won't need to obsess about the small stuff.

Perimeter-weighted irons showed there was a hungry market for clubs that were easier to hit, more forgiving on off-centered hits. Perimeter-weighted woods were sure to follow – except for the elemental problem that metal can be shaped and molded in ways wood cannot. It is a very difficult thing to fashion a wooden head that takes weight away from behind the center of the face and shifts it to the outside shell of the head, while remaining structurally sound, "plain in shape," and "traditional and customary in form."

Gary Adams, a salesman for a driving range supply company, noticed in the 1970s that golfers who switched to two-piece distance balls seemed to get a greater benefit from irons than they did from woods. He started tinkering with designs for a metal-headed wood, thinking the change in material would make a difference. There were several models of metal drivers in the nineteenth century, but metal-headed woods had long since been relegated to the status of driving-range clubs.

Those earlier clubheads were solid metal, some with hollowed out soles, durable but heavy. Gary Adams, with some help from others, realized that the casting process used in Ping irons could be used to create thin-walled shell-like hollow metal heads, making the heads lighter and shifting the weight to the perimeter. He promoted them as being longer and straighter, which wasn't true as compared to persimmon woods when both were hit on the sweet spot, but was true for mishits. Adams's TaylorMade metal-woods got the same benefit of increased MOI as Ping's irons. They were introduced at the PGA merchandise show in 1979 and were quickly popular on the pro Tour. Ron Streck won the rain-shortened Houston Open in 1981 using a TaylorMade driver, and Jim Simons gave the company terrific exposure by winning the 1982 Bing Crosby Pro-Am, then one of the most popular golf telecasts of the season.

TaylorMade metal-woods were roughly the same size and shape as traditional clubs. Ely Callaway had bigger visions, and ten years later he introduced the Big Bertha, which had a bigger head that spread the weight farther and increased the MOI even more. (Big Bertha had no hosel, Ely told me, because it put weight in an inappropriate location.) Other club makers followed suit and started pushing the limits of how big you could make a clubhead while keeping it light enough to swing effectively. The faces and walls got thinner to reduce the weight of the otherwise huge heads. But even steel is only so strong and can only take so much stress before it collapses, especially when it's becomes very thin and the impact forces are great..

Titanium entered the scene with Callaway's Great Big Bertha driver in 1995. Titanium is lighter than steel and stronger for the same weight, widening the universe of the designers' imagination. Drivers had grown from the 190 cc Big Bertha in 1991 to this new titanium 250 cc model in four years; it took just two years for the heads to approach 300 cc, with more and bigger models on the horizon. And despite the size increase, the Great Big Bertha was actually lighter than the steel Big Bertha had been.

Because titanium is so strong for its weight, manufacturers could make the shell, including the clubface, thinner than ever, until a strange phenomenon began to take place: The club itself actually began to help transfer more momentum when club met ball during impact. We received a call from the R&D department at TaylorMade saying that they had been running some tests on some competitors' drivers as well as their own and were getting anomalous results; the ball speed off the clubhead was greater than what they expected given the resilience of the test ball and the mass and speed of the head at impact. This could only happen if the face itself was acting like a trampoline, i.e., the losses in energy during impact were reduced.

It is almost unfathomable that a face could be made so thin that it would give way and then recover during the incredibly short time a ball is in contact with it. At impact, a force of about 1,700 pounds is exchanged in .00045 seconds. The blink of an eye takes about 0.1 seconds; there is time for 220 impacts of this duration in the time it takes for one blink. Yet titanium clubfaces were deforming and recovering during that time, propelling a ball forward with impetus beyond that of the swing speed and clubhead mass alone.

This had never been possible before. The ODS was a ball standard, not a ball-and-club standard. We had always imagined that we could control distance by controlling the ball; had the club makers found a loophole? No, because of a rule change we had suggested several years earlier, one that incorporated the principle of governing effects rather than causes.

The very first rule book statement regarding Form and Make of Clubs noted that a club head may not "contain any mechanical contrivances, such as springs." That provision was removed in 1956, presumably because the USGA had realized by then that a spring in the clubhead wouldn't do any good since impact is too short for it to deform and recover.

Once manufacturers started making metal-woods, we realized it might someday be possible for some hitherto unknown material to function like a spring, adding energy to the propelling force of impact. The old rule covered "contrivances," but if it sprang from a property of the material itself, would that word cover the situation? Also, the Wilson Reflex iron had been submitted for approval, its manufacturer claiming that it had a face that functioned like a spring. It didn't – but what if someday something did? That's why, in the 1984 reorganization and simplification of the Rules, we included in Appendix II the following:

### 4-1e. CLUB FACE

**Hardness and Rigidity:**
The club face must not be designed and manufactured to have the effect at impact of a spring which would unduly influence the movement of the ball

Nailed it! This is exactly what was happening, and we were covered for the situation because the rule describes the effect rather than narrowing itself to the causes and even suggests that we not punish the manufacturers too harshly because a full violation would require design intent. I don't think these club makers were trying to create a springlike effect, they kept making the faces thinner for weight-related, MOI-increasing reasons, and the effect just happened. They certainly sounded surprised when I called it to their attention. In one case where a major manufacturer's driver showed a clear and measurable springlike effect, the person I'd contacted denied it, but quickly added that some Japanese manufacturers did have springlike effect in their drivers and we should vigorously pursue them and enforce the rule.

Once they were aware of the situation, of course, they could no longer ignore it, and in a perfect world they would have been brought back in line with the Rules, and there would be no springlike effect engineered into today's drivers. This is not what occurred, mostly for reasons related to our prior topic, the grooves on the faces of irons.

The detailed specifications for grooves were essentially unchanged from their introduction in 1942 through the early 1980s. It is likely, however, that fewer than 40% of the clubs on the market in the '80s conformed to those specs.

The note on Markings on Clubs in Appendix III of the 1983 Rules declared that grooves had to be V-shaped. This was reasonable when the grooves were stamped or rolled into the face of a club in the final stage of the production process, as they were with forged clubs. With casting, however, the grooves would go through so many steps from start to finish that it was impossible to hold to the precise definition. Each step softens the feature details, and since the groove itself is only about the width of fifteen human hairs, it is easy to see how much precision can get lost. The process does well with larger features such as cavity-backs, numbers and club names, but the V-shape in the original model became more of a U-shape in the final product after all those steps.

There was no intent to violate the standards, and the altered grooves showed no performance advantage over V-grooves, so we took the reasonable and sensible step of permitting a groove by rule to have diverging sides and setting a maximum depth of .020 inches. The sides could meet in a V or come straight down to a flat bottom – which was not really flat based on the process – or slant equally to the flat or rounded bottom. All the other regulations regarding maximum width and spacing between grooves were unchanged.

In accordance with the new specs, Karsten Manufacturing was one of the first to take advantage of the change and intentionally design "square" grooves, as the U-shaped groove was commonly called. The edges of these grooves were relatively sharp. Tour players at the time favored balata balls, named for the latex created from the sap of a balata tree. The modern balls did not use natural balata, but rather a synthetic cover with similar properties to the soft balata latex. The sharp-edged grooves did a great deal of damage to these covers, shearing off little "threads" as effectively as a cheese grater.

In an effort to reduce the damage to the balls, Ping began to round off the edges. This action, not the shape of the original groove, was what caused a major problem. By softening those edges, and not changing the groove pitch they were reducing the distance between the grooves by widening the grooves themselves. Because they had been originally designed to the very limits of the specs, this small but real change meant that ratio of groove separation to groove width was less than permitted and the clubs were then nonconforming.

In the opinion of a PGA official who first noticed the rules violation – using a jewelers' eyepiece with an optical reticle designed to make "in field" groove measurements – and the USGA, the "land to groove width" ratio, i.e., the ratio comparing the size of the flat space between grooves to the adjacent groove width, went from the prescribed minimum of 3:1 down to about 2.3: 1. The grooves were too close together. If we allowed this, the next sets of irons would be designed to have a 2.3:1 ratio, and how could we keep the manufacturers from rounding those down further? This is an inevitable problem with not enforcing the rule as written.

By actual measurement, the groove had increased by slightly more than the width of two human hairs. There was no measurable difference in performance, but nonetheless the rule had been violated, and when we told Karsten that his groove did not conform, he insisted that it did. Karsten Manufacturing wound up filing a

$100 million antitrust lawsuit against the USGA and me personally. The issue in dispute was from what point the measurement should be made. We were fairly clear in our minds that a groove begins where there is a substantial departure from the plane of the face. This had to be defined, and I drew up a 30-degree rule, which was adopted. This stated that the groove begins where a tangent line angled at 30 degrees to the face touched the edge of the groove. This would be very close to the same place that the extremely detailed pre-1984 specification called for when measuring V-grooves with an edge radius. Ping argued that the width of a groove should be measured down the wall of the groove, which is like saying that the way to measure the size of the Grand Canyon is by noting its width when you're halfway down on your burro.

The legal process is never fun, and while the measurements involved were small, the stakes were not. Because it was filed as an antitrust case, the damages would be tripled if we lost; Karsten Manufacturing stood to gain $300 million at the USGA's expense.

The case was eventually settled without any money changing hands except for what both sides paid their lawyers. The USGA agreed to grandfather the existing nonconforming clubs that were manufactured prior to the settlement; all Ping Eye2s made between 1985 and March 1990 are considered conforming regardless of any subsequent rules changes. Ping agreed to modify its groove, and marked all the new clubs with a plus sign to indicate the change had been made.

The PGA Tour in the U.S. wanted to go further. It believed that some golfers were getting undue spin out of light rough, so it tried to ban all square grooves – which are really U-shaped – on Tour, even those considered conforming by the USGA. Many Tour players used

Ping irons, and Karsten Manufacturing sued the PGA Tour to allow them to continue to use them without further modification. Ping was ultimately successful, and the Tour's proposed ban on square grooves was withdrawn.

The potential $300 million exposure for the USGA left many in the USGA hierarchy gun-shy about future battles. That attitude had significant repercussions when we faced the problem of springlike effect.

Despite the clarity of the rule – *the club face must not be designed and manufactured to have the effect at impact of a spring which would unduly influence the movement of the ball* – the manufacturers insisted that they could not be expected to follow it without a spelled-out test protocol and defined specifications. Tactics that worked so successfully before to confuse the committee were again being used. I argued to the USGA's Executive Committee, vehemently, that we had a precise definition already: *no spring-like effect*. Zero. We found several clubs, once we knew what to look for, that were clearly and obviously nonconforming. And this time, the performance effect was not trivial at all. A method to measure whether a club had a springlike effect was easy enough to develop and could readily have been enforced in the same way as the symmetry rule – by establishing intent and going back to an outright ban on springlike effect.

I warned the I&B and Executive Committee members that there would be a quantum jump in how far the professionals could drive the ball if we allowed them to use these nonconforming clubs and their offspring. We didn't know exactly how much distance they'd add, but we did know that the Overall Distance Standard would no longer be an effective limit on distance – something of major concern to the governors for a hundred years or more – once the club itself added to the propelling force. It was quickly apparent that the USGA had no stomach for another lawsuit and wanted to come up with a compromise that would grandfather in all existing clubs, writing the state of the art in 1998 into the Rules. Their solution was not unlike the ultimate Ping resolution, except that the manufacturers would be able to keep making and selling the offending clubs and perhaps try to keep pushing the limit even further.

Before long, all golfers would become familiar with the phrase "coefficient of restitution," or COR, the measure of how efficiently momentum is transferred in a collision. Let's say a ball is flung at a brick wall (solid, unmoving, and with infinite mass) at 100 mph, and it rebounds off the wall at 75 mph. The COR of that collision is the separation velocity divided by the approach velocity, or 0.75. To take a realistic scenario, say a persimmon clubhead traveling at 110 mph collides with a golf ball, which then takes off at 160 mph while the clubhead is slowed to 76 mph following impact. The COR equals separation velocity (ball speed minus head speed after impact) divided by approach velocity (head speed before impact); in the persimmon example, the COR is .764. The speed of the ball is a direct result of its resilience, with the clubhead contributing only its mass and speed to the collision. This was similar to the first generation of metal-woods and even the first titanium heads.

In our testing, we found the COR of the new titanium-faced clubs to be more like .827; the ball stays on the face longer, so the clubhead slows more, and the *oomph* from the recovering face increases the ball speed, so both elements of the separation velocity are enhanced. The committees wanted to allow all existing clubs to stay within the limit, so they proposed a COR limit of 0.83.

I believe this is an example of how science and specificity has been misused in the rule-making process. The only question we should have been answering is whether there was a springlike effect, not how large an effect might be tolerable. The laws that say "no smoking" don't add "but five or six cigarettes are OK." Nor do they bother to define what smoking is.

Once you've set a precise standard allowing an effect rather than enforcing the rule as written, you take on the burden of having to test every club with great precision in order to make and maintain a list of conforming products. This is the downside of compromising a clear and simple rule where, to effectively monitor it, you needed only a clear understanding of its intent.

Moreover, once you've decided to allow some springlike effect, I don't see why you need to set a limit at all. The administrators looked at 0.83 and reasoned, if the manufacturers can create this effect now, who knows how large the number might get in the future? What they didn't seem to realize is that there is a natural physical limit on how efficient the transfer can ever get. The theoretical limit is 1.00, but among other things, such a collision would be silent, since sound itself is an expenditure of energy. The practical limit is around 0.93, but difficult or close to impossible to get there. So, having made a decision that would lead to a nearly immediate ten-yard increase in driving distance on the PGA Tour, the committee balked at letting nature set its own limits, which would only add about another five to eight yards to the equation but would eliminate the need for costly testing, weekly listings of conforming and nonconforming drivers, and complicated and meaningless field-testing to look for violations that would neither measurably affect performance nor influence the outcome of a tournament.

Setting a limit also makes it almost inevitable that some nonconforming clubs would find their way onto the market under the guise of conforming models. There's nothing nefarious involved; it's just that a standard must include some kind of test tolerance, and the designers will soon engineer clubs that incorporate that tolerance. That would be fine if manufacturing were as precise as design, but it's not; when you design right to the edge, normal variations will put some individual clubs over the limit. The differences are trivial, but that only points to the unimportance of the actual standard.

The potential legal consequences obviously had some influence and kept the USGA from enforcing a sound and valuable rule. The downside is that, it wrote into the rules a new and complicated specification that would require monitoring and putting test procedures on file and so forth. We thus created a problem that the organization would spend fifteen years trying to solve – and would undermine its own authority in how it went about it.

As we expected, the professionals immediately began hitting the ball farther – they all switched to drivers that would give them this boost– and it wasn't long before the ball makers came out with their own magic pellet that gave the pros the distance advantage of a solid ball with the control and feel of a softer-covered one. As the distance gains mounted on the pro Tour, these same administrators decided they had to do something to stem this awful problem – even though it was a "problem" only for the elite players who make up less than 0.1% of all golfers – so they started issuing questionable regulations to try to limit the damage done by the horse we had let out of the barn.

In fairly quick succession, the USGA created rules restricting the height of a tee, the length of a club, the size of a clubhead, and the degree of forgiveness that could be built into a club as measured by MOI. None of these resulted in any decrease in distance, nor would there be a jump in distance if these new rules went away. I guess they feared that the pros would soon be averaging 400 yards per drive and were no doubt concerned that, as the USGA President put it, "the game in [the] future will be relegated to the only place where it can be played, and that is on the great prairies of our Western country." As noted in chapter one, he actually said that in 1902, but you get the idea. The laws of physics did not allow that to happen back then, and they will not allow it to happen now or in the future either.

Nonetheless, to fight this perceived problem – one of its own creation – the USGA cut off avenues that might make the game slightly easier for the average golfer by restricting the MOI and gave itself new regulatory responsibilities for testing and measuring and posting lists of conforming and nonconforming clubs.

And then, when those changes did nothing to reverse the distance gains that had already started to level off, it turned once again to the subject of grooves, with a new regulation aimed at the performance of elite golfers from the rough. Beginning in 2011, new clubs must be manufactured to meet the following newly restrictive groove specs added to those that already existed:

- Grooves must have a plain cross section.

- For clubs other than driving clubs, the cross-sectional area of a groove divided by the groove pitch must not exceed 0.0030 square inches per inch (0.0762 mm²/mm). [To explain: This limits the proportion between the area of the groove in cross section and the combined size of the groove width and the area between grooves; it decreases the cross-sectional area of the groove by about 40% as compared to the previous specs.]

- For clubs whose loft angle is greater than or equal to 25 degrees, groove edges must be substantially in the form of a round having an effective radius which is not less than 0.010 inches (0.254 mm) when measured as shown in Appendix II of the Rules, and not greater than 0.020 inches (0.508 mm). Deviations in effective radius within 0.001 inches (0.0254 mm) are permissible. [This places a specification on how rounded the edges of a groove must be, keeping them from being too steeply sharp; squarer edges help the clubface put spin on the ball by making it harder for grass to come between the edge and the ball. The loft angle specified is roughly that of a modern 4-iron, bringing nearly all irons and some hybrids under the rule.]

These changes are aimed directly at the best players, particularly on the professional level, who are believed to be putting too much spin on shots from light rough, i.e., grass about 1.5 to 2 inches long. The stated goal is to put more of a premium in high-level play on driving the ball in the fairway. The hope is that golfers will choose to forego maximum distance in order to avoid hitting into the rough, since they would have less control over their shots from there with the revised grooves on their clubs. It is a backhanded attempt at reducing distance, but it will eventually affect all golfers – if nothing else, their old clubs will eventually become nonconforming – most of whom don't need this restriction. As a Condition of Competition, a tournament can require all players to use clubs that conform to these rules beginning in 2010; the PGA and LPGA Tours have done so for its events, and the USGA will for its Open Championships as well.

Other golfers may continue to use their existing (nonconforming) clubs until 2024; this is intended to keep the average golfer from having to buy new clubs right away, figuring he's likely to get new irons sometime in the next fourteen years anyway. Manufacturers may not make clubs with the old groove configuration after December 2010. Notice that this change requires the USGA to create and maintain another cumbersome list of conforming and nonconforming clubs, irons this time.

If the ruling bodies want to encourage players to drive carefully, rewarding accuracy at least as much as length, there are surely less intrusive ways to do so than to make a rule – the first roll back in the history of equipment rule making – that affects everyone. Creative course setup for elite tournaments would do the job nicely. Micromanaging the specifications has become a bad habit and a process that never should have started in the first place.

The issue really is, Is this necessary? Is there really a problem of such import that it justifies the disruption? Have we not once again overreacted to a perceived problem?

The unfortunate result of the explosion of scientific knowledge in the last forty years has been an excessive zeal on the part of regulators to make larger and larger intrusion into smaller and smaller matters. The golfer who is ultimately responsible for making sure the equipment he uses conforms with the rules is unable to do so without accessing a huge database, and even then there is some doubt and confusion. Officials are equally confused, as the process of determining conformity becomes ever more cumbersome. It's hard to see the big picture in a microscope and hard to get the right answers when you're asking the wrong questions. Intent and effect are the cornerstones of a sounder, simpler approach.

# CHAPTER THREE

## The Rules Today

The Rules of Golf may often feel as if they are handed down from on high, but they do change, breathe, evolve, and respond to the game.

Sometimes it takes experience with a faulty rule change for the main bodies to see the error of their ways. At various points over time, for example, the R&A and USGA have experimented with lesser penalties for out of bounds or a lost or unplayable ball, reducing them from stroke and distance to distance alone. In the 1950 Open Championship at Troon, Roberto de Vicenzo was playing the short par-three eighth hole, known to the world as "Postage Stamp" for its tiny green. He hit his tee shot into a tough lie in a bunker; rather than face a difficult recovery, he declared his ball unplayable and played again from the tee, hitting his second shot near the pin, and made his putt for a par. His second tee shot was a fine shot, and everything he did was completely proper and within the rules, but it was certainly not how the rules makers believed the game should be played. They only had themselves to blame, and the stroke-and-distance penalty was restored soon after.

In the early twentieth century codes issued by the R&A and echoed by the USGA, the rules for stroke play and match play were separate, and the organization of the material was otherwise largely haphazard. New rules would be added to the end of a particular section, regardless of how they related to the ones already on the books.

As we've seen, the first regulations covering equipment came in a clause held separate from the rules themselves and titled "Form and Make of Clubs." This first appeared in the USGA rules in 1909 (the R&A version appeared a year earlier) and was joined in 1920 by a second clause, "The Limitation of Ball," which listed the maximum weight and minimum size for a golf ball, noting that the ruling bodies "will take whatever steps they think necessary to limit the power of the ball with regard to distance, should any ball of greater power be introduced."

In 1934, the very first paragraph of the rules stated, "The Game of Golf consists in a ball being played from the 'Teeing Ground' into the 'Hole' by successive strokes, with Clubs and Balls made in conformity with the directions laid down in Clause on 'Form and Make of Golf Clubs and Balls.'" This was the first reference to the Form and Make clause within the main body of the rules and the first time balls were included as well. "The Limitation of Ball" was renamed "Weight and Size of Ball."

In the history of the organization of the Rules of Golf, there are three critical twentieth-century dates. The first is 1946, when the rules of match play and stroke play were combined for the first time in the USGA rules. (The R&A lagged behind on this, not yet ready to give up on some match-only rules, such as the stymie.) The Form and Make clause was now headlined "Rules Governing Form and Make of Clubs and Balls," making explicit that these were to be treated with the force of rules.

The second vital date is 1952, when the first joint rules were issued by the USGA and the R&A in concert. Representatives of both organizations' Rules Committees labored for several years to iron out their differences and put together a unified set of rules. The

R&A gave up the stymie and also its ban on center-shafted putters; the size of the ball remained a point of departure between the two, with the R&A insisting the smaller ball was vital for play under the windy links conditions on its side of the Atlantic.

In this revision, the Form and Make clause became Rule 2: Form and Make of Clubs, the first time it was included in the numbered body of the Rules of Golf. Rule 3 covered Weight, Size and Velocity of Ball, the initial velocity test having been added by the USGA in 1942.

With the USGA and R&A working together, rules changes and revisions were essentially put on a four-year cycle, the two Rules Committees getting together in conjunction with the Walker Cup matches. A few small changes might be issued in an interim edition, but the two bodies agreed to publish their full revised rules quadrennially.

The third major date is 1984, publication date of the most significant revision of the rules since the first joint edition. For decades, finding the applicable rule for a given situation was a challenge, and those who could do so even with a book in hand were highly prized. William J. "Bill" Williams led the drive to rewrite and reorganize the entire rule book, putting the rules together in a logical progression, organized by subject. At the same time, we simplified the language of the rules themselves, eliminating outmoded terms and archaic word order. Our hope was that it would be easier for the golfer to make his way through the rules, increasing the chance that he might actually read and follow them.

The primary Rules that cover equipment are Rule 4, Rule 5, and (to a lesser extent) Rule 14. In this chapter, I will review them closely, along with the two official appendices that are referred to in them and contain most of the important details. All wording that appears in the centered sections comes directly from the Rules of Golf.

### Clubs and the Ball

The United States Golf Association (USGA) reserves the right, at any time, to change the Rules relating to clubs and balls (see Appendices II and III) and make or change the interpretations relating to these Rules.

## RULE 4. CLUBS

A player in doubt as to the conformity of a club should consult the USGA.

A manufacturer should submit to the USGA a sample of a club to be manufactured for a ruling as to whether the club conforms with the *Rules*. The sample becomes the property of the USGA for reference purposes. If a manufacturer fails to submit a sample or, having submitted a sample, fails to await a ruling before manufacturing and/or marketing the club, the manufacturer assumes the risk of a ruling that the club does not conform with the *Rules*.

### Definitions

All defined terms are in *italics* and are listed alphabetically in the Definitions section.

The section begins with a note or caveat for the player, advising him to consult with the USGA (or R&A in their version) if he has any doubt about whether his clubs conform to the Rules. Anyone who's spent even a few seconds looking at Appendix II will understand why there might be doubt. The onus is on all players to be sure their clubs conform, but really, what one should do is to purchase them from a reputable manufacturer or contact the USGA.

The rest of the preamble is directed at the manufacturer and designer and is mostly there to try to protect the USGA from damage claims if and when a club is ruled to be nonconforming. It is a strongly worded warning to check with the organization and get a ruling before putting anything into production.

The Rule itself starts at 4-1, Form and Make of Clubs – a title that has not changed since the first reference to equipment in the rules in 1908-09.

### 4-1. Form and Make of Clubs

#### a. General
The player's clubs must conform with this Rule and the provisions, specifications and interpretations set forth in Appendix II.

**Note:** The Committee may require, in the conditions of a competition (Rule 33-1), that any driver the player carries must have a clubhead, identified by model and loft, that is named on the current List of Conforming Driver Heads issued by the USGA.

Before we started getting so overly specific about clubs in the early 1970s, this rule (which was then Rule 2: The Club and the Ball) described the general, basic characteristics of a club: Shape of Head, Attachment of Shaft, Nature of Grip, etc., along with the specific prohibitions discussed in previous chapters (traditional and customary; no mechanical contrivances; no concavity; plain shaft; no moving parts; and so on). This was usually enough for a golfer to determine if his clubs conformed; the statement about checking if you were in doubt appeared at the end of the rule. The old rule also made reference to detailed specifications for markings on the clubs, which were issued to manufacturers and appeared in the Appendix.

The Note in 4-1(a) reflects the USGA's – and the R&A's in its version – modern role as arbiter of all equipment for significant competitions. It has taken on the burden of testing every driver clubhead submitted and listing those that conform in all their abundant details. The list has to include every variation of every permissible head, and if the list has been adopted as a condition of competition, you must be certain the exact markings on your clubhead are noted on the list. If your club conforms, but has never been submitted for testing, you can safely use it as long as the Committee has not adopted this condition of competition. (A "condition of competition" is a special rule adopted by the Committee running the competition. Certain "conditions of competition" are recommended for all USGA and R&A events – professional, elite amateur, local and state qualifying events, but not generally regular club competitions. This divide, and the use of "conditions of competition" in general, creates a semi-bifurcation of the Rules between elite and average golfers going back to the mid 1970s, a circumstance that was written directly into the Rules in the 2010 groove changes.)

When trying to make sense of the cumbersome hole the administrators have dug for themselves, it is important to clearly understand that the difference between conforming and nonconforming clubs is not a matter of life and death. Slight violations don't necessarily make any measureable performance difference, and championships won't be won or lost on the basis of a club's conformity, unless someone's using an obvious and outlandish piece of equipment – a club with a gyroscope, a sighting device, mirrors, interchangeable parts, and so on.

### b. Wear and Alteration

A club that conforms with the Rules when new is
deemed to conform after wear through normal use.
Any part of a club that has been purposely altered
is regarded as new and must, in its altered state,
conform with the Rules.

Rule 4-1(b) deals with the effects of wear and tear and has obvious
application to grooves and grips. If a new grip has indentations to
indicate where to put your fingers, that is a violation of the rule that a
grip cannot be molded for the hands. If it happens naturally through
wear and use, that's OK as long as it conformed when it was new.
Similarly, if a clubface becomes slightly concave through long years
of wear, it is still conforming. This is a sound rule and the only way
to administer it.

The second sentence is particularly important for grooves. It is
possible, through erosion over time, that the rounded edges of a
groove might extend so that the space between grooves becomes too
small to be conforming. The first sentence tells us that the club is
still OK; however, if you have your clubs regrooved or milled, those
deliberate alterations mean the grooves must be considered new, and
so they must conform in their altered state to whatever specifications
are in effect at the time of alteration. We have good reason to believe
that a worn groove does not provide any advantage nor, in fact, does
any worn part as long as the user was the wearing party as in the case
of an indented grip into which you place your fingers, because this is
where they have been all along during the wearing process.

The general intent of 4-1(b) is that if a club conforms when new,
it will always conform and does not need to be rechecked. Thanks to
rules like the 2010 groove change, which is the first rollback in the

history of equipment performance rules, this long-standing premise is no longer necessarily true.

### 4-2. Playing Characteristics Changed and Foreign Material

#### a. Playing Characteristics Changed
During a *stipulated round*, the playing characteristics of a club must not be purposely changed by adjustment or by any other means.

#### b. Foreign Material
Foreign material must not be applied to the club face for the purpose of influencing the movement of the ball.

If you could change the playing characteristics of your club, it would be the equivalent of having more than fourteen clubs in your bag. Rule 4-2(a) illustrates the Challenge objective: You are supposed to cope with different conditions through your ability, not just by altering your equipment.

The clause on foreign material should be self-evident; if we're going to the trouble to make rules about equipment, you can't suddenly add something new that changes the way equipment works.

"Foreign material" doesn't only mean a manufactured material. I had a friend who would take a practice swing in the long grass next to the tee just before hitting his drive. He was a friend, but this and a few other incidents led to a parting of the ways. If you intentionally rub grass on the face of your club to influence the movement of the ball, knowing full well that there's a rule against "foreign material," you're violating the rule even if what you're doing is completely ineffectual. The rule deals with intent: "*for the purpose* of influencing the movement.*" Adding moisture by rubbing the face in long, succulent grass for the purpose of influencing the movement of the ball is no different than moving the ball out of a divot.

### *PENALTY FOR CARRYING, BUT NOT MAKING STROKE WITH, CLUB OR CLUBS IN BREACH OF RULE 4-1 or 4-2:

**Match play** -- At the conclusion of the hole at which the breach is discovered, the state of the match is adjusted by deducting one hole for each hole at which a breach occurred; maximum deduction per round – Two holes.

**Stroke play** – Two strokes for each hole at which any breach occurred; maximum penalty per round – Four strokes.

**Match or stroke play** – In the event of a breach between the play of two holes, the penalty applies to the next hole.

*Any club or clubs carried in breach of Rule 4-1 or 4-2 must be declared out of play by the player to his opponent in match play or his *marker* or *fellow competitor* in stroke play immediately upon discovery that a breach has occurred. If the player fails to do so, he is disqualified.

### PENALTY FOR MAKING STROKE WITH CLUB IN BREACH OF RULE 4-1 or 4-2: Disqualification.

There is a distinction between carrying and using a nonconforming club; if you merely carry it, the penalty is analogous to that for carrying more than fourteen clubs (Rule 4-4). If you use it, you're disqualified. This is a change that was made relatively recently – the old penalty was disqualification for either carrying or using

– and I like it. I agree that disqualification is correct for using a nonconforming club. It would be even better if it was easier for the player to make a reasonably informed decision about his own clubs based on either an interpretation of the rules himself or some visible stamp of approval on the club. I will discuss this later.

### 4-3. Damaged Clubs: Repair and Replacement

#### a. Damage in Normal Course of Play

If, during a *stipulated round*, a player's club is damaged in the normal course of play, he may:

(i) use the club in its damaged state for the remainder of the *stipulated round*; or

(ii) without unduly delaying play, repair it or have it repaired; or

(iii) as an additional option available only if the club is unfit for play, replace the damaged club with any club. The replacement of a club must not unduly delay play and must not be made by borrowing any club selected for play by any other person playing on the *course*.

**Note:** A club is unfit for play if it is substantially damaged, e.g., the shaft is dented, significantly bent or broken into pieces; the clubhead becomes loose, detached or significantly deformed; or the grip becomes loose. A club is not unfit for play solely because the club's lie or loft has been altered, or the clubhead is scratched.

The crucial phrases here are "in the normal course of play" and "without unduly delaying play." If you break the shaft of your putter because you were leaning on it while waiting for your partner to putt, you may (i) continue to use it for the rest of the round, presumably gripping it at the point where it broke; (ii) tape the broken pieces together if you have tape with you and can do so without holding up play, which replacing the shaft would do; or (iii) send your caddie to the pro shop or locker room (or zip in yourself at the turn) and get a replacement, as long as the putter is so badly damaged that it is deemed unfit for play.

If you're lucky enough to damage the club badly enough at a point in the round where you won't need it any more, e.g., if you only use it for the tee shot on one particular par-three, you may replace it with any conforming club, not merely an undamaged version of the same club. This doesn't make too much sense to me; if you break your 4-iron, like Tiger at Augusta, by hitting a tree on your follow-through, why should you be able to replace it with a lob wedge? But the rule says you can: "*any* club." The original must, however, be "unfit for play," a fairly high standard that should be obvious to any observer.

### b. Damage Other Than in Normal Course of Play
If, during a *stipulated round*, a player's club is damaged other than in the normal course of play rendering it non-conforming or changing its playing characteristics, the club must not subsequently be used or replaced during the round.

If, instead of breaking your 4-iron on your follow-through, you broke it by smashing it into that tree in frustration, Rule 4-3(b) says you're out of luck. You can't replace it, and you can't use it with the bent or broken shaft or other damage that affected the playing characteristics. You did it to yourself, and the Rules are not going to help bail you out.

### c. Damage Prior to Round

A player may use a club damaged prior to a round, provided the club, in its damaged state, conforms with the *Rules*.

Damage to a club that occurred prior to a round may be repaired during a round, provided the playing characteristics are not changed and play is not unduly delayed.

### PENALTY FOR BREACH OF RULE 4-3b or c:
Disqualification.

However you damaged the club in a previous round – in the normal course of play or in a fit of temper -- if you like how it plays and it still conforms with the rules, you can put it in your bag and use it. Several types of damage may make a club nonconforming, however: a bent shaft, a putter whose loft is now more than ten degrees, etc. Your clubs must conform at the start of a round.

A friend of mine, Lou Riccio, who was also a colleague on the handicap research team – I was responsible for directing handicap research and assembled and directed an impressive group of overly qualified but avid golfers who helped develop the Slope and GHIN (Golf Handicap and Information Network) System – played with a putter with a bent shaft. The shaft had become bent by accident, and he continued to use it despite my urging him not to; in my mind, even though the club had been damaged accidently, it shouldn't conform for use in subsequent rounds. This was not the rule at the time, as long as the club was not bent on purpose or in a fit of temper. For at least two years I argued with P. J. Boatwright – Executive Director and supreme rules guru, rules maker, and interpreter for more than a quarter of a century and a good friend – about this violation of common sense. He wouldn't budge; he accused me of trying to get the rule changed in an effort to stop the flow of winnings to my colleague with the bent-shafted putter. Logic ultimately prevailed, and in 1984, about four years after my pleading and arguing with P.J., the rule was changed and now a club must be conforming at the start of a round.

I should have learned from this that time will eventually resolve a problem if it truly is a problem and that in some cases pushing too hard to get it done sooner than nature dictates doesn't always work and leads to unnecessary friction and frustration.

### 4-4. Maximum of 14 Clubs

#### a. Selection and Addition of Clubs
The player must not start a *stipulated round* with more than 14 clubs. He is limited to the clubs thus selected for that round, except that if he started with fewer than 14 clubs, he may add any number, provided his total number does not exceed 14.

The addition of a club or clubs must not unduly delay play (Rule 6-7) and the player must not add or borrow any club selected for play by any other person playing on the *course*.

#### b. Partners May Share Clubs
*Partners* may share clubs, provided that the total number of clubs carried by the *Partners* so sharing does not exceed 14.

#### c. Excess Club Declared Out of Play
Any club or clubs carried or used in breach of Rule 4-3a(iii) or Rule 4-4 must be declared out of play by the player to his opponent in match play or his *marker* or a *fellow-competitor* in stroke play

> immediately upon discovery that a breach has
> occurred. The player must not use the club or clubs
> for the remainder of the *stipulated round.*

The fourteen-club limit was added to the Rules in 1938. There is no requirement that a player have as many as fourteen – though a minimum of one is essential – and the player can add clubs so long as he never goes beyond fourteen. Rule 4-4 actually led to Rule 4-3 (this was not the original numbering); before there was a limit, there was no need to consider restrictions on when and how a damaged club could be used or replaced.

The penalty for breach of 4-4a or b in stroke play is two strokes per hole, to a maximum of four strokes, and loss of hole to a maximum of two holes per round in match play.

There have been more than a few examples of this penalty in professional play. In the 2001 Open Championship at Royal Lytham & St. Annes, Ian Woosnam was tied for the lead after three rounds, birdied the first hole, and discovered en route to the second tee that his caddie had put two drivers in the bag, giving him fifteen clubs. The two-stroke penalty applied to the first hole moved him out of lead; he finished four shots behind David Duval.

Johnny Miller ran afoul of Rule 4-4 in the 1976 World Series of Golf. As Miller was playing the seventeenth hole, his caddie noticed that Johnny's six-year-old son's cut-down putter, barely a foot and a half long, was down at the bottom of the bag, too short to be visible amidst his other clubs. Miller called it to the attention of some rules officials before signing his scorecard, to see if it counted towards his fourteen-club limit. Several of them just laughed it off, but as Miller related in his autobiography, one of them, Joe Black, felt differently. "Let's see," he said. "It's got a grip…it's got a shaft…

it's got a clubhead…by golly, it's a golf club!" The result was a four-stroke penalty, two each added to his score for the first two holes.

It's important to note that the penalty for a breach of 4-4c is disqualification. Golf is a game of honor, and those who choose to play it accept the responsibility that comes with that. You are expected to own up to your violations; if you knowingly fail to report the presence of a fifteenth club, you will receive the game's harshest penalty. No one other than Miller, Woosnam, and their caddies would likely have known about the extra club in their bags; neither would have considered not declaring it for even one second.

A statement at the beginning of the Rules book – at the beginning of the Section I: Etiquette – is one of the most important declarations in the book. It is entitled "The Spirit of the Game":

### The Spirit of the Game

Golf is played, for the most part, without the supervision of a referee or umpire. The game relies on the integrity of the individual to show consideration for other players and to abide by the Rules. All players should conduct themselves in a disciplined manner, demonstrating courtesy and sportsmanship at all times, irrespective of how competitive they may be. This is the spirit of the game of golf.

I like that: *The game relies on the integrity of the individual to show consideration for other players and to abide by the Rules.*

Without the spirit of the game being applied by all who participate, this game has no substance.

And yet, in one critical area, golf on the organizational level is moving away from its own ideals. That area is performance-enhancing drugs.

The ruling bodies, along with the PGA Tour, have decided that drug testing should be implemented and that it is important to let the world know that golf is clean. They've gone so far as to add the following to the listed conditions of competition in Appendix I, Part C, of the rule book:

## 10. ANTI-DOPING

The *Committee* may require, in the conditions of competition, that players comply with an anti-doping policy.

If I had to guess, I'd say it's there because of golf's efforts to get into the Olympics. I wonder if the USGA and R&A have thought about how this differs from the rest of the Rules. In nearly every other aspect of the sport, players are told their responsibilities and are expected to live up to them.

If they were concerned about drugs, the way to handle it within the traditions of the game would be to declare in the Rules that performance-enhancing substances are not permitted, and all players would be honor-bound to follow within the dictates of his or her conscience. Just as they are when they find a fifteenth club in their bag or see the ball move slightly at address.

If players cannot be trusted to follow a rule against using drugs, how can they trusted to call other penalties on themselves? How is it possible to need drug testing but not a referee or an umpire? The minute the governing bodies determine that it is necessary to test for drugs, they have fractured the essence of the game by shifting responsibility for enforcing the rules away from the players and onto a separate party. They undermine the premise on which golf is built, and gain nearly nothing in return.

## RULE 5. THE BALL

### 5-1. General

The Ball the player plays must conform to the requirements specified in Appendix III.

**Note:** The *Committee* may require, in the conditions of a competition (Rule 33-1), that the ball the player plays must be named on the current List of Conforming Golf Balls issued by the United States Golf Association.

### 5-2. Foreign Material

Foreign material must not be applied to a ball for the purpose of changing its playing characteristics.

### PENALTY FOR BREACH OF RULE 5-1 or 5-2:

Disqualification.

### 5-3. Ball Unfit for Play

A ball is unfit for play if it is visibly cut, cracked or out of shape. A ball is not unfit for play solely because mud or other materials adhere to it, its surface is scratched or scraped or if paint is damaged or discolored.

If a player has reason to believe his ball has become unfit for play during play of the hole being played, he may lift the ball without penalty, to determine whether it is unfit.

#### Before lifting the ball...

It's so much easier with the ball. Its properties, like those of the clubs, are defined in an Appendix, and the one you use must conform. Most of the things that can go wrong with it involve its going into a hazard, being hit out of bounds, being lost, and so on – and these are not equipment rules, they're the rules of the game itself. You are what the position of the ball says you are, either in the hole or underwater.

The list of conforming balls is a condition of competition, not a part of the Rules; it does not apply unless the committee declares it so in advance. In most club-level or non-championship events, there is no reason to use this list, any more than the list of conforming driver heads.

I once heard from a lady who had won a competition at her home club using a golf ball made by Spalding and bearing a Mickey Mouse logo. A day or two after the competition was over, some of the other ladies pointed out that this ball was not on the conforming golf ball list, implying that she had either cheated or had some unfair advantage. She was very disappointed that a ball she had used, manufactured by Spalding and with a Mickey Mouse logo – both reputable companies – would be nonconforming. I assured her that the ball undoubtedly met all the required specifications, and unless the list of conforming balls had been posted for the competition she was not in violation. There are thousands of specialty advertising golf balls produced every year that are not intended to be used in major competitions; the USGA does not place a ball on the list unless requested by the manufacturer, and Spalding had no reason to think the ball should be listed. This is an example of how the conforming ball list can be misused.

Rule 5-3 continues for four more paragraphs, one penalty provision and two notes. At one time, this rule was important in resolving the thorny problem of balls that split into pieces. Before the twentieth century, gutta-percha balls would often break apart. Some nineteenth century codes directed that a broken ball could be replaced with a new one at the place where the largest piece lay. When the wound ball became standard in the early 1900s, the problem pretty much went away, and this provision was eliminated from the rule.

In 1976 with solid balls becoming popular, a reference to broken balls was reinserted, and the paragraph covering them now reads as follows:

> If a ball breaks into pieces as a result of a *stroke*, the *stroke* is cancelled and the player must play a ball, without penalty, as nearly as possible at the spot from which the original ball was played.

We will return to the ball when we get to Appendix III.

## RULE 14. STRIKING THE BALL

### 14-1. Ball to be Fairly Struck At
The ball must be fairly struck at with the head of the club and must not be pushed, scraped or spooned.

A great old rule. Golf requires that you *strike* the ball, distinguishing it from hockey or shuffleboard. You can hit the ball with any part of the head – no pool-cue maneuvers, please – but the specifications in Appendix II governing design of clubs make it difficult and/or inefficient to hit the ball with anything but the face of the club, and make sure that the club only has one face (to protect the intent of the fourteen-club rule).

### 14-2. Assistance
In making a *stroke*, a player must not:

**a.** Accept physical assistance or protection from the elements; or

**b.** Allow his *caddie*, his *partner* or his *partner's caddie* on or close to an extension of the *line of play* or the *line of putt* behind the ball.

**PENALTY FOR BREACH OF RULE 14-1 or 14-2:**
MATCH PLAY – Loss of hole; STROKE PLAY – Two strokes.

You cannot have your caddie hold an umbrella over you or line you up and stay behind you through the stroke. This is why you see caddies on the LPGA Tour move away from the player before she swings; I don't know why it's considered OK for a professional golfer to have her caddie advise her on her alignment for every shot, but that's a different question. In the Decisions book, there is a question about whether a player may hold an umbrella himself during a stroke, as when he's tapping in a short putt. The answer is yes, because 14-2 is about receiving *assistance,* and the player holding an umbrella themselves is not being assisted.

At the Masters a few years ago, Phil Mickelson arrived at the eighteenth tee, and his caddie placed his bag beside the tee marker. The bag's shadow turned out to be exactly where Mickelson teed his ball. Player and caddie both insisted that this was a coincidence, and so there was no breach of the rule; if the bag had been positioned for the purpose of casting that shadow, it would be a violation. Assistance requires intent, and if there is no intent (and only the player and caddie know for sure), there's no penalty.

### 14-3. Artificial Devices, Unusual Equipment and Unusual Use of Equipment

The United States Golf Association (USGA) reserves the right, at any time, to change the Rules relating to artificial devices, unusual *equipment* and the unusual use of *equipment*, and make or change the interpretations relating to these Rules.

A player in doubt as to whether use of an item would constitute a breach of Rule

14-3 should consult the USGA.

A manufacturer should submit to the USGA a sample of an item to be manufactured for a ruling as to whether its use during a *stipulated round* would cause a player to be in breach of Rule 14-3. The sample becomes the property of the USGA for reference purposes. If a manufacturer fails to submit a sample or, having submitted a sample, fails to await a ruling before manufacturing and/or marketing the item, the manufacturer assumes the risk of a ruling that use of the item would be contrary to the *Rules*.

Except as provided in the *Rules*, during a *stipulated round* the player must not use any artificial device or unusual *equipment*, or use any *equipment* in an unusual manner:

**a.** That might assist him in making a *stroke* or in his play; or
**b.** For the purpose of gauging or measuring distance or conditions that might affect his play; or
**c.** That might assist him in gripping the club, except that:

(i)   plain gloves may be worn;
(ii)  resin, powder and drying or moisturizing agents may be used; and
(iii) a towel or handkerchief may be wrapped around the grip.

**Exceptions:**

**1.** A player is not in breach of this Rule if (a) the *equipment* or device is designed for or has the effect of alleviating a medical condition, (b) the player has a legitimate medical reason to use the *equipment* or device, and (c) the *Committee* is satisfied that its use does not give the player any undue advantage over other players.

**2.** A player is not in breach of this Rule if he uses *equipment* in a traditionally accepted manner.

**PENALTY FOR BREACH OF RULE 14-3:**
Disqualification.

**Note:** The *Committee* may make a Local Rule allowing players to use devices that measure or gauge distance only.

The phrase "or use any *equipment* in an unusual manner" was added in 2008, as was the exception for players with medical problems. *Equipment* is defined in Section II:

> *"Equipment"* is anything used, worn or carried by the player or anything carried for the player by his *partner* or either of their *caddies*, except any ball he has played at the hole being played and any small object, such as a coin or a *tee*, when used to mark the position of a ball or the extent of an area in which a ball is to be dropped. *Equipment* includes a golf cart, whether or not motorized.
>
> **Note 1:** A ball played at the hole being played is *equipment* when it had been lifted and not put back into play.

**Note 2:** When a golf cart is shared by two or more
players, the cart and everything in it are deemed to be
the *equipment* of one of the players sharing the cart.

If the cart is being moved by one of the players (or
the *partner* of one of the players) sharing it, the cart
and everything in it are deemed to be that player's
*equipment*. Otherwise, the cart and everything in it are
deemed to be the *equipment* of the player sharing the
cart whose ball (or whose *partner's* ball) is involved.

We have strayed away from the club and ball and now have to
consider other items and issues. The USGA is trying to protect
itself in the preamble, preempting possible legal challenges and
consequences. Wrist bands, compasses, gloves, earphones, tees, head
gear with blinkers – all fall under *equipment* and if you want to
market some new model you'd be smart to run it by the USGA first.

In the mid 1970s, this rule simply referred to artificial devices
that might assist the player in making a stroke or in his play and
also banned distance-measuring devices. As it grew longer and more
complex, including more specifics and "unusual equipment," it has
increasingly resembled something put together by some legal minds.
"Tradition" and "unusual manner" are difficult to define precisely,
but a real golfer knows when he has violated the intent of such clauses
and if not he should seek advice from a committee and accept the
decision. They are only difficult to enforce when someone is trying
to push the envelope of what's acceptable and when someone is not
prepared to take the responsibility of making a decision based on
common sense. If the consequences of an unusual decision will cause
potential conflict, then those who experience conflict on a daily basis
will interfere with what makes sense and attempt to avoid the conflict

by drafting additional language for the rule even though the conflict may infrequently arise. This unnecessarily complicates the rules and moves away from allowing an expression of an understanding of the games fundamentals.

For this reason, Exception 2 is a breath of fresh air, a sign that the rules makers are moving toward trying to explain their intent and let that be the governing principle. Exception 1 is also a case where intent is vital, and the committee is left to judge whether the disabled person is getting an unfair advantage through a special device.

I believe that as 14-3 became more specific and covered "unusual equipment," it should have been moved to Rule 4: The Club. This would have made it unnecessary to repeat the preamble about consulting with the USGA that appears in Rule 4 and also here in Rule 14-3 (not Rule 14, mind you, just 14-3).

"Plain gloves" means no bumps or lumps to help position the club in your hands, or Velcro to help in gripping the club. This is a good example of a provision that can be waived by a committee under Exception 1. Special devices such as attachments designed for use with a prosthesis or thick and bulging grips and gloves with wrap-around straps for arthritic golfers wouldn't be permitted in the U.S. Open but ought to be allowed on a case by case basis by the committee for a club-level event.

The note regarding a Local Rule permitting distance-measuring devices was added in 2008. This was a logical and indeed inevitable change that came about because golfers were using such devices every day and there was no earthly reason to ban them. It makes no sense to say that you can get yardage from a caddy or a sprinkler head but not from a handheld GPS device. I don't know why they didn't simply alter the Rule itself to permit measuring devices and add a Local Rule that these can be barred as a condition of competition. It's only a matter of time before they're authorized for use on the PGA Tour and in USGA events.

One of the more ridiculous rulings of recent years doesn't appear in the numbered rules or in any of the appendices. In an effort to crack down on long driving, the USGA decided to put a limit on how high you can tee the ball by restricting the length of a tee. There was no sensible place to put such a rule – other than the circular file – so it was added to the Definition of a tee in Section II:

### Tee

A "tee" is a device designed to raise the ball off the ground. It must not be longer than 4 inches (101.6 mm), and it must not be designed or manufactured in such a way that it could indicate the *line of play* or influence the movement of the ball.

Notice that last phrase and remember it the next time some product hits the market with the claim that it is more effective than the traditional tee and will add yards to your drive. By definition, a tee must not influence the movement of the ball. If the new tee "works," it's nonconforming; if it's conforming, that's because it has no effect.

Whenever you put a limit into a rule – like the four-inch limit on a tee – it all but guarantees that manufacturers will try to get as close to the limit as they can. After all, the closer you get, the more it must help your game; the limit is there for a reason, right? "Why?" is a very good question when thinking about many of the recent equipment rules changes.

## APPENDICES II & III

The USGA/R&A reserve the right, at any time, to change the Rules relating to clubs and balls and make or change the interpretations relating to these Rules. For up to date information, please contact the USGA or refer to *www.usga.org*.

Any design in a club or ball which is not covered by the Rules, which is contrary to the purpose and intent of the Rules or which might significantly change the nature of the game, will be ruled on by the USGA.

The dimensions and limits contained in Appendices II and III are given in the units by which conformance is determined. An equivalent imperial/metric conversion is also referenced for information, calculated using a conversion rate of 1 inch = 25.4 mm.

## APPENDIX II -- DESIGN OF CLUBS

A player in doubt as to the conformity of a club should consult the USGA.

A manufacturer should submit to the USGA a sample of a club to be manufactured for a ruling as to whether the club conforms with the Rules. The sample becomes the property of the USGA for reference purposes. If a manufacturer fails to submit a sample or, having submitted a sample, fails to await a ruling before manufacturing and/or marketing the club, the manufacturer assumes the risk of a ruling that the club does not conform with the Rules.

> The following paragraphs prescribe general
> regulations for the design of clubs, together
> with specifications and interpretations. Further
> information relating to these regulations and their
> proper interpretation is provided in "A Guide to the
> Rules on Clubs and Balls."
>
> Where a club, or part of a club, is required to meet
> a specification within the *Rules*, it must be designed
> and manufactured with the intention of meeting
> that specification.

We're almost into the real nitty-gritty, but first, a *lot* of preamble, nearly all of it familiar from Rules 4 and 14-3. It's classic "cover your butt" language aimed at avoiding lawsuits, first telling the player to check with the USGA if he has any doubt about his equipment, then warning manufacturers that they had best be sure their products are conforming before they start mass production. And what if the criteria change, as they have with the grooves as discussed in Chapter 2? No problem for the ruling bodies: The preamble to the preamble reserves "the right, at any time, to change the Rules relating to clubs and balls (see Appendix II and III) and make or change interpretations relating to these Rules."

Beginning in the 1950s and continuing through the 1970s, it was extremely difficult to find anything in the rule book, because whenever new rules were added they were tacked onto the end of the list. Most of the regulations dealing with equipment were in Rule 2; 2-2 was Form and Make of Clubs and 2-3 contained the specs for balls. There was an appendix headed "Markings on Clubs," which detailed the grooves and punch marks that were permitted. Another, "Nature of Grip," showed examples of conforming and nonconforming grips.

These were in somewhat simplified form, intended for golfers as opposed to the more detailed versions provided to manufacturers.

In the 1984 reorganization of the Rules, the details were spelled out in the appendices, which have now grown from just over four pages in 1976 to fourteen pages in 2010. Some of the material in the appendices is extremely technical, and it is difficult to imagine that a golfer can use the information to determine whether or not his equipment is conforming.

For the USGA's internal use, I found it necessary, for the sake of making consistent decisions and where necessary to help innovators with questions, to develop a "Guide to the Rules on Clubs and Balls" in 1998. That guide is now available on the USGA website, www. usga.org/Rule-Books/Rules-on-Clubs-and-Balls/Equipment-Rules. We tried to move away from specifics and toward more general statements and consideration of intent. If you intend to create a grip with a bulge and a waist, it does not matter whether or not anyone would be able to spot them on inspection; you have violated the rule on grips. In the Appendix II preamble, this is expressed in the valuable last paragraph: "Where a club, or part of a club, is required to meet a specification within the *Rules*, it must be designed and manufactured with the intention of meeting that specification."

The danger of publishing the guidelines on the website is that they are not the Rules, and may tend to take the place of the Rules in an official's mind. In the introductory passages to the guide, we described the evolution of a principle from Guideline to Rule as follows:

> *Guidelines - Are used to help us interpret a Rule consistently. Guidelines are deemed to be needed when an interpretation of the Rule is queried on more*

*than a few occasions, and/or a precedent setting
decision is made. This would occur infrequently.*

*Decisions - A decision should be drafted for inclusion
into the Rules of Golf when a guideline is having to be
given out frequently (more than a half dozen times a
year), to assist with the interpretation of a Rule.*

*Rules - A Rule should be drafted if frequent reference
needs to be made to a decision on the Rules of Golf.*

The guide includes advice on interpreting the rules and specifications and notes on Field Procedures for officials. The conclusion to that last portion is particularly important:

*The vast majority of golf clubs conform to the Rules
and, therefore, equipment conformance questions
are rare. However, questions do arise from time
to time and officials need to know how to deal
with them. It is important to remember that it is a
player's responsibility to play with conforming clubs.
He cannot shift this responsibility to the officials....
In giving Duration of Competition or Duration of
Round Answers, officials in doubt should err towards
deeming clubs to conform. Disqualifying a player for
carrying a club that later turns out to be conforming
is a more serious error than allowing the use of a
club which later turns out to be non-conforming.*

Amen to that. The rules cannot cover every possible innovation or situation. The more specific you are, the more you imply that anything not specified is okay. Players are expected to observe the spirit of the game and not regard the Rules as an opportunity to search for loopholes. Is it too much to ask that manufacturers consider equipment rules the same way? So long as we focus on intent, we can identify the important principles and not waste time on silly little regulations.

### Appendix II-1

### 1. Clubs

### a. General

A club is an implement designed to be used for striking the ball and generally comes in three forms: woods, irons and putters distinguished by shape and intended use. A putter is a club with a loft not exceeding ten degrees designed primarily for use on the putting green.

The club must not be substantially different from the traditional and customary form and make. The club must be composed of a shaft and a head and it may also have material added to the shaft to enable the player to obtain a firm hold (see 3 below). All parts of the club must be fixed so that the club is one unit, and it must have no external attachments. Exceptions may be made for attachments that do not affect the performance of the club.

This opening is wonderfully simple and encapsulates much of what was in the original equipment rules, particularly "traditional and customary form and make." Generality is flexible and useful, but lawyers prefer specificity that leaves little room for interpretation. Such detail may solve the immediate problem while introducing others farther down the line.

Notice that clubs are distinguished by their shape and not by the material used to create them. Some golf commentators refer to a player hitting a "3-metal," when the proper term remains "3-wood" even if we'll never see a wooden head again.

Prior to 1983 there were different dimensional specifications for woods and irons; we determined that this was unnecessary, and so we combined the two and used the more liberal specs – the ones for woods – for both. This simplified matters, since we could now refer to the implements as clubs and putters. The phrase "attachments that do not affect the performance of the club" allows you to put lead tape on the club; increased weight on the head does not create the kind of performance change referred to in this rule.

### b. Adjustability

All clubs may incorporate mechanisms for weight adjustment. Other forms of adjustability may also be permitted upon evaluation by the USGA. The following requirements apply to all permissible methods of adjustment:

(i) the adjustment cannot be readily made;

(ii) all adjustable parts are firmly fixed and there is no reasonable likelihood of them working loose during a round; and

(iii) all configurations of adjustment conform with the Rules.

During a stipulated round, the playing characteristics of a club must not be purposely changed by adjustment or by any other means (see Rule 4-2a).

Until 1972, a club could not be adjustable at all; at that time, an exception was made for adjusting the weight of the club. I was opposed to changing the later rule to allow the types of adjustments now permitted because I felt it would make the rules more complex to understand, implement, and monitor during a round. There has always been a prohibition against changing the playing characteristics during a round, so why tempt the golfer with an adjustable club?

The R&A believed that making the change would benefit some small manufacturers and keep a club pro from having to carry a large inventory of clubs that differ only by small adjustments for lie, loft, weight, etc.; the USGA decided to go along. The current, very much more expansive rule was adopted in 2008.

We can't say that allowing adjustable clubs has done any harm – or much good. It gave the manufacturers something new to market, but I haven't heard of many golfers who change the combinations of weight or loft or lie very much. This may change as market forces take over, looking for innovations that push the limits. For most, having an adjustable driver – one was sold with twenty-six different permutations! – is like having a compass and winch on your Jeep when the only off-road experience you ever have is when you drive into your garage.

The way it has worked out, permitting adjustable clubs has allowed players to have their clubs fitted more easily, and once that's done, the adjustable-but-fixed club is OK for play. As long as everyone understands that you can't make changes during a round, the rule takes away a prohibition that didn't have to be there in the first place. That's a good thing.

### c. Length

The overall length of the club must be at least 18 inches
(0.457 m) and, except for putters, must not exceed 48 inches (1.219 m). For woods and irons, the

measurement of length is taken when the club is lying on a horizontal plane and the sole is set against a 60 degree plane as shown in Fig. I. The length is defined as the distance from the point of the intersection between the two planes to the top of the grip. For putters, the measurement of length is taken from the top of the grip along the axis of the shaft or a straight line extension of it to the sole of the club.

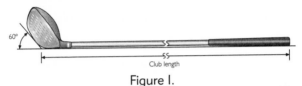

Figure I.

The initial restriction on the length of a club was intended to keep it from being too *short*. We wanted to eliminate the nuisance of what was called the "Kneel and Pray Putter," a 6-inch-long club that could only be used successfully in a kneeling position. It was silly, and the method left objectionable knee-prints on the greens. This style was objectionable – not really golf – and we proposed an eighteen-inch limit that was added to the rules in 1989. There was no need to be specific regarding the measurement of the putter length, as it was generally understood how to make a length measurement of a club and half an inch one way or the other is not going to create a problem.

Having dealt with the menace of tiny putters, I'm afraid we missed the boat on the long ones. They first appeared on the scene in the mid 1980s. I argued to the Equipment Standards Committee (which was the name of the Implements and Ball Committee from 1987 to 1990 – and a better name, if you ask me) that these clubs were nontraditional and that we should place an upper limit on the length of a putter. My concern was, and is, that by anchoring the top end of the grip to the body, you completely eliminate one degree of freedom from the stroke (up and down motion), and a fixed pivot point method of putting (one fixed point against the body, and one arm going back and through) takes wrist motion out of the stroke as well, eliminating a second degree of freedom and the error associated with it, i.e., eliminating sources of error.

Using a long putter is a more efficient way to putt, but it is considered by many a nontraditional stroke. We have used restrictive dimensional specifications in the past to discourage or make it awkward to use the club in a nontraditional manner rather than trying to specify how a club may be used. This would have been the case if we restricted the length of a putter to about thirty-eight inches.

As reported by the chair of the Committee in his 1989 annual summary, "After considerable discussion the Equipment Standards Committee decided to permit the use of the long putter. The putter was not considered to be a threat to the game even though the style is somewhat unconventional."

In July 1989, Orville Moody won the USGA's Senior Open using a long putter. A month later, the USGA and R&A put out a statement affirming that the putter was conforming and would continue to be so. Some didn't want to brand Moody as having won a championship with a club that was immediately banned. We've been stuck with it ever since. And allowing the long putter created a precedent that makes it difficult to justify outlawing other equipment for being "nontraditional."

There is no restriction on the length of a putter, which changes the game, but there is a limit on the length of the other clubs, which doesn't do anything worthwhile. In a seeming overreaction to some distance gains off the tee, the USGA put in the 48-inch limit to prevent golfers from using a 50-inch driver that is difficult to control at best and demonstrates that the length of a driver is probably self-limiting anyway. In this case, in an effort to be proactive, the USGA made a rule that only affects a few septuagenarians who may have decided to buy a 50-inch driver to match their putter or those who are trying to get bragging rights about the bunker they haven't been able to clear for years and don't mind putting dozens of shots in the weeds for every one that gives them a thrill and a story they'll tell for months.

Of course, having established a standard which is self-limiting anyway, the rules makers found it necessary to describe the precise method of measurement to make sure no nefarious 48 ¼-inch drivers slip by. The limitation in meters is 1.219. So another ninety words and a nice little sketch get added to the rules. Well done!!

How would it be – if a length limit was important – to say rather that "A club, other than a putter, may not exceed 48 inches in length"? Most of us know how to make the measurement to within plus or minus 1/4 of an inch. The point is unless it is critical we do not have to overcomplicate the rule. How straight is "straight"? Or, how long is "no longer than…" before it becomes obvious or may make a difference?

### d. Alignment

When the club is in its normal address position the shaft must be so aligned that:

i.   the projection of the straight part of the shaft on to the vertical plane through the toe and heel must diverge from the vertical by at least 10 degrees (see Fig. II). If the overall design of the club is such that the player can effectively use the club in a vertical or close-to-vertical position,

> the shaft may be required to diverge from the
> vertical in this plane by as much as 25 degrees;

The purpose of this regulation is to make it all but impossible to make a true pendulum stroke with the shaft vertical. The restriction originally applied just to putters, and it was a good change to include all clubs so that chippers could not use a pendulum stroke either. Just in case, the overall sole design is such that if it can be used effectively with the shaft in a vertical plane, the USGA can make this determination on a case by case basis.

> ii. the projection of the straight part of the shaft
> on to the vertical plane along the intended line
> of play must not diverge from the vertical by
> more than 20 degrees forward or 10 degrees
> backward (see Fig. III).

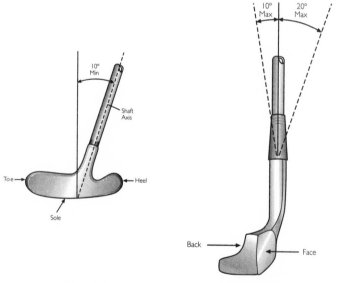

Figure II.                    Figure III.

Except for putters, all of the heel portion of the club must lie within 0.625 inches (15.88 mm) of the plane containing the axis of the straight part of the shaft and the intended (horizontal) line of play (see Fig. IV).

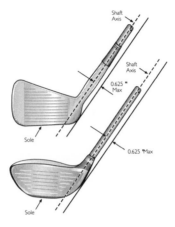

Figure IV.

The reason to limit the forward and backward angle of the shaft is to prevent putters – with all their exceptions under the rules – from being used as chippers. By rule, a putter is a club designed to be used on the green and must not have a loft of greater than 10 degrees. The heel restriction keeps clubs other than putters from creeping towards a centered shaft.

## 2. Shaft

### a. Straightness

The shaft must be straight from the top of the grip to a point not more than 5 inches (127 mm) above the sole, measured from the point where the shaft ceases to be straight along the axis of the bent part of the shaft and the neck and/or socket (see Fig. V).

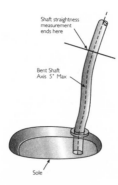

Shaft straightness
measurement
ends here

Bent Shaft
Axis 5° Max

Sole

Figure V.

The shaft has to be straight for most of its length, but is permitted to bend as it gets within 5 inches of the sole of the club. This allows a certain amount of gooseneck near the head, particularly with putters. The offset shafts in putters before the mallet-style putter, which puts significant bulk of the head behind the face, were an attempt to move the weight or center of gravity (CG) of the head far behind the shaft axis. This helps in making a more consistent stroke as the CG of the head is dragged or pulled into the impact zone.

### b. Bending and Twisting Properties

At any point along its length, the shaft must:

i.　bend in such a way that the deflection is the same regardless of how the shaft is rotated about its longitudinal axis; and

ii.　twist the same amount in both directions.

A simple and direct rule that sets an absolute standard and requires no complicated testing. It's as clear as "no springlike effect."

Unfortunately, it's being treated the same way. Despite the clarity of the regulation and its purpose – to keep the shaft free from any potential trickery by guaranteeing it twists and bends symmetrically, ensuring that some clever future designer can't build in a correction for a golfer's swing flaw – the I&B Committee made a subsequent judgment that I philosophically disagree with and that, to my mind, bends the rule itself.

The Committee was approached by an innovator who designed a method to measure how much a shaft differs from the intended symmetrical properties, identifying the axis of maximum difference so he could (under his patented method) orient the shaft to alter the performance of the club. He claimed his intent was to merely neutralize the effects of a bad, i.e., asymmetrical, shaft, the result of inevitable variations in the production process. The Committee decided to allow him to use and market his method – even though any shaft that might benefit from this analysis is, by definition, nonconforming! Perhaps the Committee felt he was providing a consumer service, compensating for the shortcomings of a shaft manufacturer's quality control. Maybe they believed that the performance differences once the shaft was "properly" oriented were minuscule or nonexistent (which they almost certainly were). Still, this creates an unhealthy precedent; allowing golfers to take advantage of an anomaly in production as though the shaft were intended to be asymmetrical comes perilously close to permitting the marketing of a nonconforming product.

The intent of the rule could not be clearer. It is, nonetheless, a fact that variations in the production process may produce asymmetries within a certain small tolerance. Once you allow people to commercially exploit those unintentional variations, you open a large can of worms. How much difference is too much? How much is acceptable tolerance, and where does performance enhancement begin? Once you start asking those questions, you're well on your way to another set of hyper-detailed specifications, another subject for elaborate and expensive testing, and another list of conforming and nonconforming components. A tough call to let it be, and a good call, rather than to be too specific without justification.

A company once tried to exploit a similar situation involving golf balls. While Appendix IIIc requires a ball to perform as though it were spherically symmetrical, and for the most part it does, perfection is all but impossible to achieve in any physical production process. Golfers can find the asymmetrical axis of their balls by floating them in a solution of salt water, noting and marking the divergence of the geometric center with the center of its mass.

This company acquired golf balls and through a balancing process identified those that were asymmetrical. They painted a line on each ball, identifying the axis of asymmetry, and advertised the fact these balls would perform in an asymmetric manner and described a method of placing the ball on the green so the weight bias would not push it off line. The information about the ball's properties could also be used to counter a slight break in the green. This commercially available ball was ruled to be nonconforming for violating the symmetry rule.

Why was a manufacturer punished for doing something the golfer could do for himself? Because the manufacturer was taking an unintentional variable and making it a deliberate aspect of the product. He was consciously marketing a product that was nonconforming by virtue of the attribute emphasized in his marketing. This was a violation of the intent of the rule. This is very different from a golfer noting the slight error in a product that was intended to be symmetrical and conforming.

There is a crucial difference between tolerance and toleration. The fact that there must be a slight tolerance for asymmetry due to the imperfection of the manufacturing process does not mean that we must tolerate efforts to exploit it. I believe that we messed up on this one with shafts.

### c. Attachment to Clubhead

The shaft must be attached to the clubhead at the heel either directly or through a single plain neck and/or socket. The length from the top of the neck and/or socket to the sole of the club must not exceed 5 inches (127 mm), measured along the axis of, and following any bend in, the neck and/or socket (see Fig. VI).

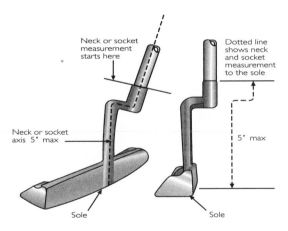

Figure VI.

Exception for Putters: The shaft or neck or socket of a putter may be fixed at any point in the head.

The original point of the attachment clause was to eliminate center-shafted clubs that were thought to provide an advantage – including putters in the R&A rules, but not in the USGA's. There is no evidence that center-shafted clubs do provide any advantage, but in this case –

as in others during our continuous review of the rules – we considered it better to leave a rule in place if it was doing no harm, making a change only if there was a good reason for the change.

The 5-inch limit was arbitrary, based on the actual length of iron hosels, but once set, it required details about how to measure it; in 1984 we added further interpretation regarding the measurement because some designers were offering convoluted neck designs for various reasons, e.g., to use as an alignment aid over the ball). This is a good example of how additional specs within a rule can result from either inconsistent interpretations through the years or submission of many designs with the same violation. Is there a way to deal with this one without adding a relatively simple measurement method to the specs? I doubt it.

With regard to this particular rule, I recall seeing Tiger Woods at one event on TV (I don't recall if it was in the pro-am or on the first day of the event) using a putter with a neck that looked like it was considerably longer than five inches. I called the manufacturer to ask about the club design; the next day there was a weld mark in the neck of the putter, and it was measured and was found to conform.

Could he have been disqualified for the violation? Yes, but that seems excessive for a minor unintentional infraction that conferred no advantage. I prefer the way it was handled: It was immediately corrected, and the manufacturer was warned to check this specification in all its models. Once on notice, they knew they would not be treated as gently in the future. I would like to think that the USGA would have done the same thing if the golfer involved were ranked 137th in the world instead of first.

### 3. Grip (see Fig. VII)

The grip consists of material added to the shaft to enable the player to obtain a firm hold. The grip must be fixed to the shaft, must be straight and plain in form, must extend to the end of the shaft and must not be molded for any part of the hands. If no material is added, that portion of the shaft designed to be held by the player must be considered the grip.

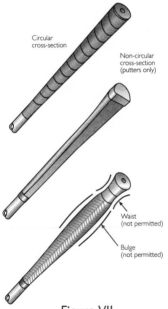

Circular
cross-section

Non-circular
cross-section
(putters only)

Waist
(not permitted)

Bulge
(not permitted)

Figure VII.

i.  For clubs other than putters the grip must be circular in cross-section, except that a continuous, straight, slightly raised rib may be incorporated along the full length of the grip, and a slightly indented spiral is permitted on a wrapped grip or a replica of one.

ii. A putter grip may have a non-circular cross-section, provided the cross-section has no concavity, is symmetrical and remains generally similar throughout the length of the grip. (See Clause (v), below.)

iii. The grip may be tapered but must not have any bulge or waist. Its cross-sectional dimensions measured in any direction must not exceed 1.75 inches (44.45 mm).

iv. For clubs other than putters the axis of the grip must coincide with the axis of the shaft.

v. A putter may have two grips, provided each is circular in cross-section, the axis of each coincides with the axis of the shaft, and they are separated by at least 1.5 inches (38 mm).

The first grip rule was added in 1947. It stated, simply, "The grip shall consist of a plain extension of the shaft to which material may be added for the purpose of obtaining a firmer hold."

A year later, the USGA determined that some manufacturers were creating grips that were molded to the hands, providing improper assistance, so some restrictions were added: "The grip shall be a continuation of the shaft to which material may be added for the purpose of obtaining a firmer hold. The grip shall be substantially straight and plain in form, may have flat sides, but may not have a channel* or a furrow* for the fingers or be molded to the fingers. *The above prohibition against a channel or a furrow for the fingers will not become effective until January 1, 1949."

Between 1948 and 1983, the rule changed very little, except to indicate that a player could not use any artificial device that might assist him in making a stroke or in his play or, not being part of the grip, be designed to give him artificial aid in gripping the club. An exception by special note allowed the player to wear a glove and to add a material or substance such as tape, resin, or gauze to the grip. (This reference was shifted, appropriately, from the nature of the grip to the rule on Artificial Devices in 1976.)

We decided to modify the grip rule slightly for the 1984 revision, removing the specific reference to channels and furrows from the body of the rule and to be very clear as to the intent in the appendix:

i.   For clubs other than putters, the grip must be generally circular in cross-section, except that a continuous, slightly raised rib may be incorporated along the full length of the grip.

ii.  A putter grip may have a noncircular cross section provided the cross section has no concavities and remains generally similar throughout the length of the grip.

iii. The grip may be tapered but must not have any bulge or waist.

iv.  The axis of the grip must coincide with the axis of the shaft except for putters.

I was very proud of this change, as it said what it meant and was difficult to misinterpret. There are always designers who try to find or create a loophole in the rules to their own advantage. The more specific the rule is, the easier it is to do this. The clearer you can make the intent, the stronger the rule will be.

Some of the specifics came about as a result of the preferences of some committee members. The "reminder rib" is permitted because some insisted it was a traditional thing. Many golfers put a thin cord beneath the under-listing before wrapping the grip; the rib provides a reminder of where to place their hands to square the face at address.

But how big could such a rib be? Some had tried to get away with a coat hanger wire or even a wooden dowel; those were far too big, and we had to spell out the distinction in the guidelines, though not in the rule itself. The same is true of the later indentation for simulated wrapped spiral grips.

The flat-sided pistol grip was permitted as some committee members insisted it was traditional. By coincidence, it was what the Executive Director at the time had on his putter, but it was also very common. A putter can be gripped in many different ways, few of which are critical and none necessary to keep a firm hold on the club, which is not the case with full iron and wood shots. Did this exception matter in the scheme of things? No, it didn't, but it was an exception and exceptions cause problems in interpretation of a relatively simple rule based on intent.

Part (iv) came about because of a Karsten Solheim design. He thought a center-shafted iron would be more efficient; it wouldn't, and there was already a rule against it. So he subsequently put a bend in the shaft under the grip in 1967, arguing that the grip and the shaft are two different things. Other manufacturers then tried to achieve a similar effect with a molded grip; we added the restriction that the axis of the grip had to coincide with the axis of the shaft, (except for putters) and that took care of it.

We found that some manufacturers were making extra-wide grips for putters, some two or three inches across, to enable golfers to place their hands opposite each other rather than one up and one down or overlapping . This was intended to help the golfer not break his wrists during the stroke. We considered this an improper advantage, and so we added a maximum size for the cross-section. The introduction of the long putter required the addition of a clause permitting the split grip simply because no manufactured grips were long enough to accommodate this style of putting. It was important that the two grips be separated by a significant gap, because two tapered grips that abutted would form a waist. The two grips had to be circular in cross section, because otherwise their flat sides could be oriented on the shaft to function as if the grip as a whole was molded to the hands. (This last restriction cost Taylor Smith a spot in a playoff against Tiger Woods at the 1996 Disney World Classic; he was tied for the lead after seventy-two holes, but one of the two grips on his long putter had a flat side.) These changes were incorporated in 1992.

## 4. CLUBHEAD

### a. Plain in Shape

The clubhead must be generally plain in shape. All parts must be rigid, structural in nature and functional. The clubhead or its parts must not be designed to resemble any other object. It is not practicable to define plain in shape precisely and comprehensively. However, features which are deemed to be in breach of this requirement and are therefore not permitted include, but are not limited to:

(i) All Clubs

- holes through the face;
- holes through the head (some exceptions may be made for putters and cavity back irons);
- facsimiles of golf balls or actual golf balls incorporated into the head;
- features that are for the purpose of meeting dimensional specifications;

- features that extend into or ahead of the face;
- features that extend significantly above the top line of the head;
- furrows in or runners on the head that extend into the face (some exceptions may be made for putters); and
- optical or electronic devices.

(ii) Woods and Irons

- all features listed in (i) above;
- cavities in the outline of the heel and/or the toe of the head that can be viewed from above;
- severe or multiple cavities in the outline of the back of the head that can be viewed from above;
- transparent material added to the head with the intention of rendering conforming a feature that is not otherwise permitted; and
- features that extend beyond the outline of the head when viewed from above.

"Plain in shape" took the place of "traditional and customary." As we approached the 1984 revision, the USGA decided to examine all the clubs that had been deemed nonconforming by violating the traditional and customary clause. We were looking for common attributes but couldn't find any. So the USGA came up with this new phrase instead, "plain in shape."

In a world where golfers are always seeking something new, designers and marketers will do anything to distinguish their new club as being different. Different and new is assumed to be better.

The manufacturer may know that it is just an aesthetic change to distinguish the product from the competition and may not make any significant difference to performance, but as golfers we are inclined to buy hope and we are easily distracted by a style change. Is this not a part of the charm of golf, and if so, how much should the USGA restrict innovation that isn't performance-based?

The rule in general is to provide guidance, and a little more specifically to try to define the boundaries of what's acceptable. Tradition is a guide, but many things that are commonplace today would have been unthinkably untraditional a hundred years ago. "Traditional and customary" should be reserved for radical changes, not incremental ones.

The rules protect the good of the game in many ways. They need to allow for innovation and shouldn't stifle it, but one of the traditions of the game is a certain amount of dignity, and they can help prevent someone from making a mockery of golf itself. A clubhead must resemble a clubhead; it cannot be shaped like a cartoon character. We do not want Nike making clubs that resemble a swoosh. It's okay for a putter to remind you of a frog, but you can't put nonstructural, nonfunctional pieces like flippers or webbed toes on it. Maybe suggesting that the profile should be generally smooth would eliminate the need to be specific about features.

Once again, the danger of listing forbidden features is the implication that anything not listed is permitted. The most pertinent parts of the rule are the first two sentences – *plain in shape* and *structural and functional*. The rest of it is basically reactive, addressing some innovations that had been attempted and trying to anticipate what else might come along.

The original 3-Ball Putter had three balls in a row behind the clubface. This made the clubhead very deep from front to back, so the designer put an extra-wide fin on the back in an effort to make it conform (the heel-to-toe distance must be greater than from face to back). This fin was for the sole purpose of meeting dimensional specifications. It was not part of or near to the face, i.e., the toe /heel. This one putter begat two rules clauses, though it seems strange to allow white ball-sized discs but not facsimiles of a golf ball.

The ban on optical or electronic devices should probably be the first example listed. We don't want anyone even thinking that such stuff belongs in the game. A club with any sort of electronic device externally attached or integrated into the design is a good example of an inappropriate intrusion into the game and a wonderful example of where the true meaning of "traditional and customary" can effectively be used without question.

The USGA had long allowed slits and slots in the head of a wood – the classic Hogan driver had a "speed slot" on the outside – but rather than get into a lot of extended arguments about how what kinds of nontraditional shapes might be described as having "slots," we put in the prohibition on cavities that are visible from above and vertical holes in the head. I think that this is where more thought was needed as it started a slippery process toward too much specificity that may not have been necessary by trying to cover a specific innovation that could have been ruled on otherwise.

The club that led to this particular clause was the Bullet Hollow Point Driver, whose C-shaped clubhead had a severe cavity in the back. The mouth of the cavity was considerably narrower than the cavity itself, in an attempt to avoid the existing prohibition on clubs with a hole through the head. When does a hole become a hole? How small an opening is big enough? This wasn't an argument we wanted to have – the makers of the Bullet did want to have it and filed a lawsuit when their club was ruled to be nonconforming – so we closed the potential loophole by making reference to visible cavities rather than just holes. And of course we had to spell out that you couldn't put a transparent sheath on top and claim it wasn't a cavity. This is typical of the hoops you have to jump through when the rules become too specific. If we'd stopped with the words "plain in shape," and put the interpretations into the guidelines, we would be in a much better position and would keep from cluttering the rule book with unnecessary verbiage.

It really would be smarter and better to keep everything focused on intent and general principles and to have the guts to stand by them. The rules can only be enforced in USGA events or by those who choose to do so. You can play using a bow and arrow, but it is not golf.

### b. Dimensions, Volume and Moment of Inertia

(i) Woods

When the club is in a 60 degree lie angle, the dimensions of the clubhead must be such that:

- the distance from the heel to the toe of the clubhead is greater than the distance from the face to the back;

- the distance from the heel to the toe of the clubhead is not greater than 5 inches (127 mm); and

- the distance from the sole to the crown of the clubhead, including any permitted features, is not greater than 2.8 inches (71.12 mm).

These dimensions are measured on horizontal lines between vertical projections of the outermost points of:

- the heel and the toe; and

- the face and the back (see Fig. VIII, dimension A); and on vertical lines between the horizontal projections of the outermost points of the sole and the crown (see Fig. VIII, dimension B). If the outermost point of the heel is not clearly defined, it is deemed to be 0.875 inches (22.23 mm) above the horizontal plane on which the club is lying (see Fig. VIII, dimension C).

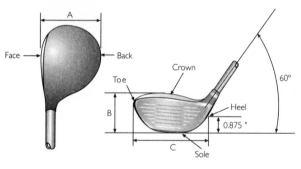

Fig. VIII

The volume of the clubhead must not exceed 460 cubic centimeters (28.06 cubic inches), plus a tolerance of 10 cubic centimeters (0.61 cubic inches).

When the club is in a 60 degree lie angle, the moment of inertia component around the vertical axis through the clubhead's center of gravity must not exceed 5900 g cm (32.259 oz in), plus a test tolerance of 100 g cm (0.547 oz in).

(ii) Irons
When the clubhead is in its normal address position, the dimensions of the head must be such that the distance from the heel to the toe is greater than the distance from the face to the back.

More than any other, this section of the rules is aimed at defining and protecting what is "traditional in form and make" for clubs. How big? What proportions? What rough shape?

The first issue goes back to the very early days of club regulations. The head of a golf club is wider than it is deep; this distinguishes it from a croquet mallet (as discussed in Chapter One). The R&A and USGA may or may not have recognized that the club design they outlawed with the words "mallet-headed type" in 1910 was probably superior to the one everyone had been using, since it moved the center of gravity back in the head, away from the face. Most likely it was their simple horror at the unconventional nature of such clubs that led to the regulation; whatever you wished to say about the cylindrical Simplex clubs, they were surely untraditional.

In trying to rationalize this, I find it hard to accept the reason for some of these restrictions. "Heel to toe...not greater than five inches" – why not? If a club designer can somehow jump through all the other hoops put in his way, and do so with a 6- or 8- or 12-inch clubface, why shouldn't he be able to? Many of these restrictions are self limiting. The USGA is being unnecessarily proactive here in an effort to control distance – even if it won't admit it, there is no evidence that clubhead size adds distance for the professional or long hitter – or to demonstrate its own relevance. It is cutting off harmless future innovation rather than waiting for it and then judging it, case by case, using sound guidelines such as not being plain in shape or being nontraditional. It provides exact measures, but no clear science that demonstrates there is any advantage to equipment that goes beyond the limits. I believe it's more useful – and honest – to call a club nontraditional or not plain in shape than to make up arbitrary dimensional specifications and then have to monitor them and develop and list a precise methodology by which to make the measurement.

If you have a size limit, do you really need a volume limit? If you have a size and volume limit, do you really need a limit on moment of inertia?

I have an idea for clubs that may solve some of the dilemmas addressed above: If the club floats, then it doesn't conform. A driver with a head size of about 270 cc will be at the limit, taking into account the shaft volume, grip weight, and specific gravity, as well as the head weight, which is self-limiting. Throw it into the water and if it sinks it's OK. Call it the Witch Rule.

What if – some of the committee legal minds might opine – an innovator finds some less dense water mixture trying to prove his club is the best because it only just sinks (this therefore must be the best or the USGA would not have adopted this rule). Instructions to the staff would be to specify the density of the water and define floating and the rate of sinking when the barometric pressure and temperature is appropriately adjusted for average conditions at Far Hills or St. Andrews and include this in the rule. A list would then be needed to identify those clubs that floated and were considered non-conformers. This would comfortably place the Witch Rule firmly alongside other unnecessarily overcomplicated rules.

More importantly, do you need any of those limits at all?

Since the 1920s, there have been very precise limits on the size of grooves or punch marks in the rule book, yet we got along without a limit on clubhead size until 2004. We understand that clubheads grew alarmingly between 1991 (the 190 cc Big Bertha) and 2002 (several 500 cc models submitted to the USGA for approval), but this was not a progression that could possibly continue. The size of a driver's head is naturally limited, primarily by the player's ability to swing and control it, secondly by his ability to find a headcover. At the 460 limit ultimately enacted, the gains from COR and MOI had largely maxed out; it would be pointless to create a 600 or 700 cc driver, since the improvement would be trivial and the extra cost of materials substantial. The USGA and R&A couldn't even agree on the reason for a volume limit: The R&A said it was to control distance, while the USGA claimed that such oversized drivers were not traditional. (Of course, neither were the ones they allowed in.) The volume limit was originally going to be 385 cc, but howls of outrage from manufacturers whose clubs had already been judged conforming persuaded the USGA to raise the limit to 460 (actually 470 including the 10 cc tolerance).

If the goal is to reduce distance, a size limit makes little sense. Maximum distance comes from hitting the ball on the sweet spot of the clubface, which is something the longest hitters – the elite golfers, including Tour pros – already do very well. They would not be much affected by increasing the effective size of that sweet spot. The average golfer, whose distance off the tee is no threat to the game or its courses (windows and windshields are another matter), is the main beneficiary of the larger sweet spot created by a bigger clubhead. By putting restrictions on clubhead size and MOI, the USGA made the game potentially harder for the vast majority of players, without taking anything away from the best golfers – the exact opposite of how the organization should think.

I'm not quite sure why woods and irons could not be covered under the same rule as they have in all other cases, therefore (ii) Irons is unnecessary.

### (iii) Putters (see Fig. IX)

When the clubhead is in its normal address position, the dimensions of the head must be such that:

- the distance from the heel to the toe is greater than the distance from the face to the back;

- the distance from the heel to the toe of the head is less than or equal to 7 inches (177.8 mm);

- the distance from the heel to the toe of the face is greater than or equal to two thirds of the distance from the face to the back of the head;

- the distance from the heel to the toe of the face is greater than or equal to half of the distance from the heel to the toe of the head;

- the distance from the sole to the top of the head, including any permitted features, is less than or equal to 2.5 inches (63.5 mm).

For traditionally shaped heads, these dimensions will be measured on horizontal lines between vertical projections of the outermost points of:

- the heel and the toe of the head;

- the heel and the toe of the face;

- the face and the back;

and on vertical lines between the horizontal projections of the outermost points of the sole and the top of the head.

For unusually shaped heads, the heel to toe measurement may be made at the face.

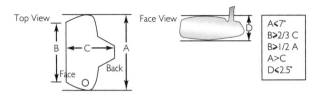

Figure IX.

Reads a bit like one of those intelligence tests, doesn't it? "If Joe is older than Pam, and Pam is half as old as Dick, and Ted will be double Joe's age when Pam turns 40...."

It is, however, wise to remember that the golfer is responsible for playing with conforming equipment and he must first resolve this riddle to have some degree of confidence that an overly officious official is not going to take him off the course for having a nonconforming putter because B< ½ A.

These various limits and proportions are much more specific than they need to be. For most of the dimensions involved, there are no performance benefits if you go beyond the limits – and I dare anyone to look at the putters on the market today and tell me that the rules have protected any traditions of the game.

Putting is hard enough already; as long as a putter has no moving parts or artificial aids and is plain in shape based on internal guidelines, do we need any other restrictions? I am in favor of preserving some of the traditions and basic dimensions of length versus breadth, but anything beyond this is questionable. Yes, there are some necessary restrictions, but they must be very carefully considered and not included simply to make a occasional decision easier but rather to spell out the intent and guide innovators. We must always remind ourselves that millions of golfers follow the rules voluntarily and the clearer the intent of such rules, the more they will be understood and more effectively applied. Mass acceptance and application is of the utmost importance. In specific instances where there is a genuine concern at the elite level, then a condition of competition can be used to protect the integrity of major championships.

### c. Spring Effect and Dynamic Properties

The design, material and/or construction of, or any treatment to, the clubhead (which includes the club face) must not:

i.   have the effect of a spring which exceeds the limit set forth in the Pendulum Test Protocol on file with the USGA, or

ii.  incorporate features or technology, including, but not limited to separate springs or spring features, that have the intent of, or the effect of, unduly influencing the clubhead's spring effect, or

iii. unduly influence the movement of the ball.

Note: (i) above does not apply to putters.

In 1909, Form and Make of Golf Clubs included a ban on "any mechanical contrivances, such as springs." In 1983, we altered this slightly to "the effect at impact of a spring." And the above clause is how it reads now, with the clarity of "no springlike effect" turned into the mush of "the effect of a spring which exceeds the limit set forth in the Pendulum Test Protocol on file with the USGA." The committee chairman, in my opinion, tried to justify this compromise by claiming there was no clear definition of what springlike effect was. It was like objecting to a no-smoking statute because it doesn't define "smoking."

Truthfully, as long as the clause says that the "design, material, and/or construction of, or any treatment to, the clubhead must not...unduly influence the movement of the ball," does it make any difference what else is in the rule? Lawyers may not like the imprecision of "unduly," but as a Supreme Court Justice said of obscenity, you know it when you see it.

### d. Striking Faces

The clubhead must have only one striking face, except that a putter may have two such faces if their characteristics are the same, and they are opposite each other.

At last, something simple that can be interpreted by golfers and officials alike. No getting around the fourteen-club rule by giving a single club two faces. No need to define what a "face" is or an elaborate protocol for how to count them.

## 5. CLUB FACE

### a. General

The face of the club must be hard and rigid and must not impart significantly more or less spin to the ball than a standard steel face (some exceptions may be made for putters). Except for such markings listed below, the club face must be smooth and must not have any degree of concavity.

### b. Impact Area Roughness and Material

Except for markings specified in the following paragraphs, the surface roughness within the area where impact is intended (the "impact area") must not exceed that of decorative sandblasting, or of fine milling (see Fig. X).

Illustrative impact area

Figure X.

The whole of the impact area must be of the same material (exceptions may be made for clubheads made of wood).

This clause was first introduced in 1984, but the principle had been in force for many years before that. The idea was to prevent club makers from using a soft material for putters or rubber inserts on irons to increase the spin. Now, of course, exceptions are made for putters, and spin is regulated through the "standard steel face" wording – a metallurgical version of "traditional and customary."

The original, detailed specifications for markings on iron clubs were issued in 1942. They were written by Dr. Carl Anderson of the Armour Institute and issued to manufacturers; a simplified version for the lay golfer was eventually added to the rule book. His task, as described by the chairman of the I&B committee, was "working up a set of specifications to limit the scoring to such an extent that no undue cut (spin) will be put on the ball." Anderson, who was not a golfer, discovered that this was a far more complicated process than expected because of the variety of grooves and markings then on the market, and so he essentially created a standard by observing what was being commonly used and enshrining the state of the art as the full standard.

One of the regulations was that "a reasonably-sized area of the toe and heel shall not be scored." There's no reason for this, other than the fact that that's what was done at the time. When we worked on the revision in 1983, we didn't directly overturn this, but skirted it by addressing the rule to markings in the "impact area." Material inserts in irons are presumed to be for the purpose of unduly influencing the ball and had been banned since 1931; in woods, they have traditionally been used to protect the more delicate clubhead. The exception for wooden clubs – not "woods," but "clubheads made of wood" – allows such inserts for this purpose or to be purely decorative. One manufacturer submitted a head with alternate strips of brass and wood; as long as it did not assist in putting spin on the ball, it was judged to be conforming.

When it comes to roughness, under the Club-Face clause above; "b. Impact Area Roughness and Material" states: "Except for markings specified in the following paragraphs, the surface roughness within the area where impact is intended (the 'impact area') must not exceed that of decorative sandblasting, or of fine milling (see Fig. X)."

I draw your attention to "decorative sandblasting." In 1942 the rule stated, "The face of the club shall be smooth and flat over the full surface. No sharp edges or lips due to die impression of any type will be permitted. For decorative purposes only, it is permissible to sandblast with fine sand. "

In 1976 we added a specification to this: "For decorative purposes only, it is permissible to sandblast the scored area not to exceed a roughness of 180 microinches, with a 15% tolerance. The relative roughness shall be determined in accordance with USA standards (ASA B46.1-1962) for surface texture. The direction of measurements shall be parallel to the grooves.

"The above conditions for smoothness apply to sections 2 and 3 (i.e. width of the groove and distance between grooves)."

In 1984 the USGA removed this specification from the book and kept it as a guideline for internal use. Today the area between grooves are being "laser milled" with mini grooves, and the clubs are still approved for use. Is this for decorative purposes only, or otherwise?

The USGA most likely slipped up in 1976 when – trying to be smart by identifying what it meant by roughness – we included in the rule a specification of 180 microinches with 15% tolerance to be determined in accordance with USA standards (ASA b 46.1 -1962). This has subsequently opened the door for manufacturers to work within the specs (now in the guidelines) and violate the intent of the rule. Shame on me for being part of this in 1976.

Maybe so much attention has been placed on the change to the groove rule that this detail regarding sandblasting slipped through the cracks without checking. The honor that supports the game is being lost by not developing an understanding of the intent and by being overly specific, allowing manufacturers to work around the real meaning of the rule.

### c. Impact Area Markings

- If a club has grooves and/or punch marks in the impact area, they must be designed and manufactured to meet the following specifications:

(i) Grooves

- Grooves must be straight and parallel.
- Grooves must have a plain* symmetrical cross-section and have sides which do not converge (see Fig. XI).

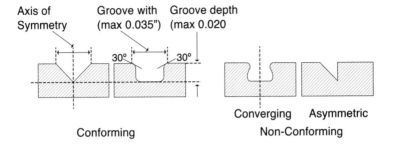

Conforming    Converging    Asymmetric
              Non-Conforming

Figure XI.

- The width, spacing and cross-section of the grooves must be consistent throughout the impact area.

- The width (W) of each groove must not exceed 0.035 inches (0.9 mm), using the 30 degree method of measurement on file with the USGA.

- The distance between edges of adjacent grooves (S) must not be less than three times the width of the grooves, and not less than 0.075 inches (1.905 mm).

- The depth of each groove must not exceed 0.020 inches (0.508 mm).

- *For clubs other than driving clubs, the cross-sectional area (A) of a groove divided by the groove pitch (W+S) must not exceed 0.0030 square inches per inch (0.0762mm²/mm) (see Fig. XII).

Figure XII

- Grooves must not have sharp edges or raised lips.

- *For clubs whose loft angle is greater than or equal to 25 degrees, groove edges must be substantially in the form of a round having an effective radius which is not less than 0.010 inches (0.254 mm) when measured as shown in Fig. XIII, and not greater than 0.020 inches (.508 mm). Deviations in effective radius within 0.001 inches (0.0254 mm) are permissible.

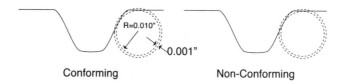

Conforming                    Non-Conforming

Figure XIII

(Two notes later explain that the specifications marked with an asterisk apply only to new models of clubs manufactured on or after January 1, 2010, and that effective January 1, 2010, the Committee may require as a condition of competition that clubs used or carried by a player must meet the asterisked specifications.)

Dr. Anderson's original specifications were quite precise, filling three pages in the rule book when they were finally published openly in 1953. Among the details:

- grooves must be V-shaped
- the side walls of the grooves must be essentially flat, and set at an angle of at least 90 degrees
- the width of the groove may not be greater than .035 inches
- the distance between grooves must be at least three times the width of the groove (to put it another way, at most 25% of the permitted area may be grooved)
- the minimum distance on the surface between the edges of any two grooves of any size is .075 inches
- the center of the grooved area may be indicated by any design as long as it fits within the boundary of a square whose sides are 3/8ths of an inch
- the total length of grooves in any one square inch of surface area may not exceed fourteen inches
- no sharp edges or lips due to die impression are permitted

This is a fine example of specificity run amok. By the time we got involved in examining grooves for the 1983 revision, *no* clubs manufactured using the investment cast process met these specs. Our choice was between banning all investment-cast clubs because they lacked V-grooves, or permitting the U-shaped groove the process could create. It was not a hard decision.

The only aspect the USGA changed was the shape of the groove, not the other specs, and it did not consider the change to be significant, though some pro golfers insisted that there was a distinct difference between the performance of cast V-grooves and cast U-grooves. A study was initiated to examine various groove configurations, under both dry and grassy conditions, with different balls to test varying cover materials. This was followed by player tests.

A difference of about 20-25% in spin rate was found between the machined U-groove and the machined V-groove when a light layer of grass intervened between the ball and the clubface. There was no difference under dry conditions. The player test verified these differences, which were reflected in how far the ball rolled on the green when hit with wedges from light rough. The scatter patterns for both groove configurations were similar, so it was considered certain that pro golfers would adjust quickly. Our conclusion was that there was a difference in performance, but that the effect on the results of tournaments would be insignificant.

The study was available to anybody who was interested; John Solheim, who was vice president of Ping at the time, said to the USGA Executive Committee that it was one of the most significant and informative studies ever performed in the game of golf.

Today, as discussed in Chapter 2, the USGA and R&A have decided – based on the opinion of Arnold Palmer and some analyzed correlation of the money list with statistics on driving accuracy – that the grooves should be changed back to V-shapes. The "square" grooves seen on Tour players' clubs are different from the U-grooves we first saw in investment-cast clubs; they are machined square using new laser milling techniques and have relatively aggressive edges. Nonetheless, it will be interesting to see if anything significant happens. From initial studies using data from the PGA Tour as the first year with the new rule comes to a close, nothing much has changed. If this trend continues to show no significant change in performance because of the groove change then we really need to examine carefully our rules-change and performance-rollback philosophy.

Some of the specifications we put into the prior rule that are still in effect were actually somewhat arbitrary. The maximum radius of 0.020 inches was introduced in 1988; we needed some measurement, because if the radius was too large you'd have a "wave" in the face rather than a groove. We settled on 0.020 because 0.01 was too small to be effectively monitored at the time. We introduced the 30-degree method at the request of the committee; we would rather have simply said the measurement where the groove starts is at the point of substantial departure from the plane of the face, but greater specificity was requested at the time. The 30-degree tangent angle made sure that the old V-grooves would conform. And as for the depth of 0.020, our groove study had shown that the most important part of the groove was the upper two-thirds.

### (ii) Punch Marks

- The maximum dimension of any punch mark must not exceed 0.075 inches (1.905 mm).

- The distance between adjacent punch marks (or between punch marks and grooves) must not be less than 0.168 inches (4.27 mm), measured from center to center.

- The depth of any punch mark must not exceed 0.040 inches (1.02 mm).

- Punch marks must not have sharp edges or raised lips.

*For clubs whose loft angle is greater than or equal to 25 degrees, punch mark edges must be

substantially in the form of a round having an
effective radius which is not less than 0.010 inches
(0.254 mm) when measured as shown in Fig. XIII,
and not greater than 0.020 inches (.508 mm).
Deviations in effective radius within 0.001 inches
(0.0254 mm) are permissible.

*...apply only to new models of clubs manufactured
after January 1, 2010...the Committee may require,
in the conditions of competition, that the clubs the
player carried must conform to the groove and
punch mark specifications above marked with an
asterisk (*)...

The punch mark specs go back to Dr. Carl Anderson as well,
updated in 2010 to add the last part about rounding the edges. Punch
marks can be twice as deep as grooves; but there are no performance
benefits to this thanks to the greater percentage of unmarked area
in the impact area (82% versus 75% for grooved clubs). The punch
mark rule should probably be withdrawn from the rules and placed
in the same barrel as the asymmetry specifications for golf balls just
in case someone decides to use punch marks again.

### d. Decorative Markings
The center of the impact area may be indicated by
a design within the boundary of a square whose
sides are 0.375 inches (9.53 mm) in length. Such a
design must not unduly influence the movement of
the ball. Decorative markings are permitted outside
the impact area.

### e. Non-metallic Club Face Markings
The above specifications do not apply to clubheads
made of wood on which the impact area of the face
is of a material of hardness less than the hardness

of metal and whose loft angle is 24 degrees or less, but markings which could unduly influence the movement of the ball are prohibited.

**f. Putter Face Markings**
Any markings on the face of a putter must not have sharp edges or raised lips. The specifications with regard to roughness, material and markings in the impact area do not apply.

We're winding down now. Decorative markings are permitted, so long as they don't influence the movement of the ball. Groove specs don't apply to clubs made of wood because such grooves are so difficult to maintain in a softer surface and don't have a great deal of effect anyway in a less-lofted club – but still, just in case, we've got the "unduly influence the movement of the ball" phrase to keep order.

As for putters – almost anything goes. The purpose of this clause was to allow soft inserts, but today there are putters with grooves designed to reduce spin; I think that's a questionable exception. It would be preferable to consider the undue influence clause on the movement of the ball as a better way to handle putters and the claims about face treatment.

## APPENDIX III - THE BALL

### 1. General
The ball must not be substantially different from the traditional and customary form and make. The material and construction of the ball must not be contrary to the purpose and intent of the Rules.

### 2. Weight
The weight of the ball must not be greater than 1.620 ounces avoirdupois (45.93 gm).

### 3. Size

The diameter of the ball must not be less than 1.680 inches (42.67 mm). This specification will be satisfied if, under its own weight, a ball falls through a 1.680 inches diameter ring gauge in fewer than 25 out of 100 randomly selected positions, the test being carried out at a temperature of $23 \pm 1°C$.

### 4. Spherical Symmetry

The ball must not be designed, manufactured or intentionally modified to have properties which differ from those of a spherically symmetrical ball.

### 5. Initial Velocity

The initial velocity of the ball must not exceed the limit specified (test on file) when measured on apparatus approved by the USGA.

### 6. Overall Distance Standard

The combined carry and roll of the ball, when tested on apparatus approved by the United States Golf Association, must not exceed the distance specified under the conditions set forth in the Overall Distance Standard for golf balls on file with the USGA.

The ball is so simple when compared to the club! It's not that there aren't variables, but they can be more easily managed; all you have to do is bypass causes and focus on effects.

The opening clause of Appendix III is music to my heart, and I believe it is a move in the right direction if only we could get away with this vagueness throughout the rule book – wishful thinking.

There has to be a rule covering size and weight to make sure everybody is playing the same game. The spherical symmetry clause is there to make explicit what we mean when we say "ball," i.e., it should perform like a ball, which we all understand to be a spherically symmetrical object. Once we developed the Overall Distance Standard, we probably could have eliminated the Initial Velocity test, but it had been a part of the rules for so long and the committee was not completely certain that it was one of the properties covered by the ODS, so we wound up keeping it. Its effects – like all others affecting distance – are of course subsumed in the ODS as they would be in an Optimum ODS.

Everybody seems to think the ball goes too far these days, at least when the pros and elite amateurs hit it. This was the case in the late 1890s after the introduction of the Haskell ball (first rubber-thread wound ball). The major rules changes to equipment recently – in the last decade or so from 1998 to 2010 – have been an attempt to reduce the distance the ball goes. In studying this cyclical mantra over the years it seems it has been taken up as a rite of passage into the halls of the USGA Executive committee. It might be more useful to try to determine whether or not a problem truly exists. I remember a president of the USGA telling me that, "The fact that there is a perceived problem is in itself a problem." The solution, however, is not to solve the perceived problem but the perception. If in fact the ball is going too far and evidence shows that the game would be better if the distance were reduced, reducing the distance – a form of suicide in today's environment – under the rules would be extremely simple: Just change the ODS to a lesser distance, and all manufacturers would have to alter their balls to keep from exceeding it.

The consequences of doing this are obvious, but few have the fortitude to propose and adopt such a change affecting 35+ million golfers, including themselves. Besides, nobody really thinks that they themselves hit the ball too far; it's always the other guy who's the problem. For over a hundred years, golfers have bought equipment because of the promise of ten more yards, or twenty. Are we really going to accept hitting the ball 10 or 20 % *shorter* without a fight? The facts are that the ball is almost locked in to a specific distance limit. I say almost because there are a few more yards left between the optimum ODS and the existing ODS. Even without changing to an Optimum ODS, there will not be any further increases in distance of any significance. Certainly there's nothing to be frightened of, so we can at last relax and use the best test lab in the world – the pro Tour – to assure us that distance has now reached a ceiling bounded only by the golfers' ability to increase head speed (which is going to be as difficult as running the marathon in less than two hours).

However, the governors of the game are still trying every which way to prevent the ball from going any farther without more restrictions on the ball itself. If they are serious about dealing with this problem, there's a direct way to do it. If you believe as I do – that the "problem" results from the efforts of a tiny percentage of golfers, and the rules should reflect the interests of all golfers and the good of the game as a whole – then the ineffectiveness of their indirect efforts is probably for the best.

As I ponder every aspect of the Rules of Golf as they apply to equipment in all their modern complexity, I find myself wondering if we've really improved the Rules so much over time. The 1941 version, under the heading "Form and Make of Clubs and Balls," contained just 332 words. It's still a template we should follow as closely as possible.

## FORM AND MAKE OF GOLF CLUBS AND BALLS

### Clubs

The United States Golf Association will not sanction any substantial departure from the traditional and accepted form and make of golf clubs which, in its opinion, consist of a plain shaft and a head which do not contain any mechanical contrivance, such as springs; it also regards as illegal the use of such clubs as those of the mallet-headed type, or such clubs as have the neck, or shaft, so bent as to produce a similar effect.

Club faces shall not embody any degree of concavity or more than one angle of loft, and shall not bear any lines, dots, or other markings with sharp or rough edges made for the obvious purpose of putting a cut on the ball. Insets in the faces of iron clubs are not allowed.

The following general considerations will guide the Rules of Golf Committee in interpreting the above:

1. The head of a golf club shall be so constructed that the length of the head from the back of the heel to the toe shall be greater than the breadth from the face to the back of the head.

2. The shaft shall be fixed to the heel or to a neck, socket or hose in line with the heel or to a point opposite the heel, either to right or left, when the club is soled in the ordinary position for play.

3. The shaft of a putter may be fixed at any point in the head between the heel and a line terminating at the center of the sole.

### Balls

The weight of the ball shall be not greater than 1.62 ounces avoirdupois, and the size not less than 1.68 inches in diameter. The Rules of Golf Committee and the Executive Committee of the United States Golf Association will take whatever step they think necessary to limit the power of the ball with regard to distance, should any ball of greater power be introduced.

There have been some good additions, such as permitting markings on the face of iron clubs. Do we really need so many others? I believe the ruling bodies would do well to sort through them and try to justify – truly justify – their inclusion. Are today's rules needed to protect the challenge the game offers? Are they making the game more enjoyable? Are they difficult to monitor? Are they overly cumbersome? Are we succeeding in avoiding litigation, and is that so important a goal? The USGA governs the game for its events, and it can do what it feels is necessary to protect the game for those championships. For everyone else, the decision to follow the USGA's rules is entered into voluntarily. Ultimately, its authority can only come from the belief of the governed that those rules make sense.

I have tried to be as bold, forthright, and constructive as possible in my commentary about the rules on equipment, many of which I was responsible for forming. I hope that all of us who love the game – a group that definitely includes the rules makers and committee members who give so much time to their organizations – can do a little introspection about exactly what it is we are trying to protect and how effective we are being in enhancing our enjoyment of the game. Golf is a bewitching, enticing game because it is such a personal challenge, and we do need order if it is to serve its purpose. It is the most wonderful game ever devised by man without divine intervention – if that is the case – and we should do whatever we can to see that it prospers and grows, spreading its benefits as far as it can go.

CHAPTER FOUR

# Making the Rules

I was walking the Atlanta Athletic Club's Highland golf course with Chris Schenkel of ABC Sports during a practice round for the 1976 U.S. Open. We were outside the ropes, following Arnold Palmer, when Sandy Tatum, then a member of the USGA's Executive Committee and soon to be the association's president, came striding across the fairway to us. "Frank, do you know what is going on here?" Sandy asked me. "Arnold is carrying three different balls and using them on different holes depending on the conditions. We have to do something about this."

Palmer wasn't doing anything wrong, nothing contrary to the Rules of Golf. What he was doing was very smart, taking advantage of something I'd noticed when testing golf balls the previous year. I was watching balls fly out of the test house onto the field, and recognized that the height of a ball's trajectory when launched about two different axes was one of the easiest ways to determine if it had symmetrical aerodynamic properties. We also measured the carry distance difference and the time in flight; all three measurements were eventually used to determine if the ball met the symmetry standard. Studying the trajectory made it obvious that different balls had very different flight properties, and under certain conditions a golfer who knew what he was doing could take advantage of a ball's characteristics. The solid two-piece balls of the time – so-called "distance" balls, generally disdained by the pros because their low-spin properties reduced their effectiveness on lofted shots – would be a good choice on long par-threes into the wind or some par-fives

•

where distance on long irons was paramount.

I sent a letter/memo (on actual paper, like we used to before e-mail) to Ken Gordon, then chairman of the I&B committee, explaining that we needed to do something about the potential effect of ball specialization. I predicted that manufacturers would soon be designing balls for specific conditions, rather than the differences just being an accidental byproduct of the production methods. In my memo to Ken, I included a cartoon drawing of a caddie, wearing a wind vane on his head and pulling a wagon with balls in separate compartments, looking into the sky in puzzlement while his pro was waiting for the best ball for the conditions on that hole. Ken enjoyed the cartoon but didn't take the issue too seriously.

So when Sandy Tatum came over to talk to me in Atlanta, I was prepared. I told him about the memo and sent him a copy the next week when I was back in the office. Sandy called and suggested that I resolve the problem. I spoke to P.J. Boatwright, the executive director, and we decided that it would be appropriate to mandate that a player could use only one ball type during a round. P.J. realized that for us to do this in the U.S. Open it would be best to get the players on board; we didn't want to offend the PGA Tour, so we conducted a survey of the players with the cooperation of and through the Tour office. We asked the players if they had tried using different balls during a round, and by far the majority said they had done so. We asked how they would react to a rule prohibiting a change of ball types during a round; about 75% said it would be a good idea or that it didn't make any difference to them. Very few thought it was unnecessary, though some just didn't vote. We passed the results on to Tour Commissioner Deane Beman, and he agreed to adopt the one-ball rule soon thereafter. This told us we were on the right track, so we simultaneously adopted the rule as a "Condition of Competition." It's not technically a rule – you can change balls on every tee if you like during your rounds with friends – but it is a condition adopted for elite competition.

We learned subsequently that Titleist already had plans to sell a sleeve of balls (I think it was a four-ball sleeve) each with different performance properties for specific conditions during a round. The adoption of the one-ball rule I believe derailed their marketing plans, and the variety pack of specialized balls never made its way to the marketplace.

It would be nice to report that the rules-making process is methodical, orderly, systematic. More often than not it's haphazard, politically driven, reactive, and dictated by the whims of the committeemen. Technical research is valuable, but it has a tough time competing with rumors, anecdotes, and gossip.

The USGA and R&A have formally governed the game throughout the world for more than a hundred years. The USGA has jurisdiction over the United States and Mexico, while the rest of the world follows the lead of the R&A. This works out to a roughly fifty-fifty split of golfers worldwide, with the balance tilting slightly toward the R&A side as more countries embrace the game.

Until the early 1920s, the USGA and R&A were in concert about the equipment rules with the exception of the center-shafted putter. Both bodies agreed their mission was to only permit the traditional and accepted form and make of clubs and were concerned about the distance generated by the new (Haskell) ball. They each put in size and weight restrictions for the ball and talked about trying to control its resilience. The U.S. body did more than just talk, putting a limit on Initial Velocity in 1942, something the R&A did not accept until 1976. (Ironically, the R&A finally agreed to an initial velocity standard the same year the USGA switched to the Overall Distance Standard; the R&A resisted the ODS until 1990.) The delay by the USGA was fueled by the lobbying of the Golf Ball Manufacturers Association, formed in 1929; the ball makers did not want to lose their ability to market their products as longer than ever. The R&A's delay reflects its belief that controlling resilience was not worth the trouble and also its reluctance to accept scientific and technical advancements that came from the upstart Americans. The R&A was confident the manufacturers would understand its viewpoint and would follow its informal guidance.

In Chapter One we saw the USGA's willingness to tinker with the size of the ball, eventually settling on the 1.68 inch/1.62 ounce specification. The R&A tested configurations other than its 1.62/1.62 standard but rejected any change for half a century after the USGA's shift. The smaller ball was vital for links play, it argued, boring through the wind with ease that the bigger American ball could not duplicate. There was probably also an element of protectionism in its resistance, since the different specs meant that American-made balls would not flood the world market. In addition, the larger ball would require more thread, increasing the British manufacturers' costs.

In 1968 the USGA and R&A formed a Joint Committee to study the feasibility of a uniform ball. The golfers on each side of the Atlantic preferred their own ball, which created a problem for European and British golfers coming to tournaments in America. Since the specification is a "no smaller than" standard, American golfers could keep using their 1.68-inch ball when they went to the U.K., but the Brits and Europeans couldn't play the 1.62-inch ball in the U.S.

The Joint Committee eventually came up with a compromise position, that everyone should adjust the standard to 1.66 inches. This made great sense to the two I&B committees, but no sense to anybody else. Manufacturers made up some prototype balls at 1.66 inches. The R&A was pleased with the playing characteristics of the new-sized ball, but the U.S. manufacturers didn't see why they should retool their plants for such a tiny change, especially since there was so little test data to show this change would make much of a difference in performance. It was a change aimed only at solving a political problem, the ongoing disagreement between the two bodies about the appropriate size and their inability to end it with a sensible solution. The U.S. manufacturers argued, reasonably, that it was silly to make everybody change rather than only one group, so why didn't they simply adopt the 1.68 standard? In a meeting at the 1973 U.S. Open, some manufacturers implied that they might pursue legal action if the compromise ball was adopted. They proposed an extensive seven-phase research program to determine the effect of such a change. The USGA recognized this as a stalling tactic but also realized their argument had merit, and so the 1.66 proposal was withdrawn. (I have the remnants of the uniform ball in my office; they were given to me by Ted Emerson, who was chairman of the I&B committee at the time of the proposal. John Salvesen, a future captain and chairman of the R&A's championship committee, was among those who tested the prototype out on the course, and he recorded a hole-in-one with it. He claims to be the only person to have scored an ace with the 1.62 inch, 1.66 inch, and 1.68 inch balls.)

The rift finally came to an end when the ball makers under R&A jurisdiction recognized that the 1.68-inch ball was becoming increasingly popular, and they were making fewer 1.62-inch balls. Even then, the R&A moved at a glacial pace. The "American" ball was officially adopted for all R&A Championships in 1983. Before the 1984 Open Championship, the R&A's General Committee declared that "thought should be given to the matter" of changing the specifications once and for all. Its I&B Committee chairman, Roger Ames, noted in his 1984 report that he was sure the British ball's days were numbered but was unsure "whether positive step should be taken by the R&A towards this end." In September 1984, Ames observed that use of the 1.62-inch ball was down to 10% in some areas but still felt there weren't strong enough reasons to change the rule. A year later, same story, same nonrecommendation. Finally, in drawing up and approving changes for the 1988 code, the R&A committed to elimination of the 1.62 ball, effective January 1, 1990.

Uniformity was ultimately more for the sake of order than for any issue of performance. It was something the administrators could rally around, showing that they were doing something. The attenuated battle demonstrated the pattern that held for most rules issues dealing with equipment: The USGA wanted action, while the R&A resisted change.

I have a great deal more sympathy with the latter position than I did when I was with the USGA. In those days, I often felt that we were the far more modern organization, using good science and taking advantage of technology to improve and better regulate the game. When we introduced the ODS, the R&A kept it out of their rules, partly because it was an American initiative and partly because they had no way of making the necessary measurements and would have had to use our apparatus. They saw this last condition as financially onerous and politically impossible.

As I look at things now, I see grounds for the R&A belief that the USGA was overreacting to innovations and adopting unnecessary standards for issues that, if left alone, would resolve themselves. In hindsight it was probably true, as today it finds itself falling into a cavern of complexity that perpetuates itself and snowballs to the point of absurdity. Golf is, after all, a game, and not a matter of life and death – contrary to what an alien might conclude by studying today's standards and the protocols used to monitor them.

Transatlantic divisions form just one of the political currents that affect the rule-making effort. The contrasts and tensions between the professional staff and the political administrators of the USGA are an ongoing source of amusement and frustration, depending on the day.

We've seen already the development of the "Let the f---ers fly" principle, as well as the tendency for the rules to reflect the preferences of particular individuals on the committee. All too often, I found, the members of the Executive Committee or chairman or the I&B committee simply did not understand the technical issues involved in making the decisions within their purview. The I&B chairmen often had neither a sound grasp of the technical standards being adopted nor of why the standards were important. If you don't understand the question, you're unlikely to come up with an answer that does much good.

The USGA Test Center is under the direction of its Senior Technical Director, who reports to the Executive Director. The researchers who work there are very capable of doing excellent studies and drawing appropriate conclusions from well-analyzed data. Too often, though, their efforts are harnessed to someone's political agenda that stems from skimpy anecdotal evidence.

The "ball goes too far" hysteria is the most visible example of this. Pro V1s and their ilk are not longer balls than the solid-core distance balls of previous generations. They meet the ODS and did so before the ODS was rewritten to express the standard at a higher clubhead speed. What is new about them is that their multiple covers make them acceptable to professional players who want more spin and softer feel on their shorter shots. The distance potential was always there, if ever a professional was willing to play Pinnacles. Combined with the springlike effect of titanium-faced drivers, the multi-covered solid ball is close to a perfect product, and thus a perfect storm for panicky administrators.

In a prior generation, the Great Dimple Race led some committee members to suggest we place a limit on the indentations permitted on the outside of a ball. Fortunately, fuller heads prevailed, sparing us the task of counting dimples and determining their depth, size, edge definition, etc. This is the type of thinking that results when nontechnical minds try to govern a technical issue; without intelligent intervention, chaos might have ensued, and the standards black hole we are approaching would have long since swallowed us up.

Sometimes all it takes to create a new rule is one creative or desperate individual. In 1967, frustrated by his putting yips, Sam Snead unveiled his "squat shot" stroke and used it to win the Senior PGA Championship. Snead insisted he could putt better by facing the hole directly, so he stood behind the ball, gripped the putter with one hand at the top and another far down the shaft, and pulled it back and through as in a croquet shot.

According to the annual report of the Implements and Ball Committee in 1967, the croquet style had been "long approved." Even so, Snead's efforts triggered a fierce debate. There were strong advocates for the style, with the President of the USGA at the time as well as a former President, an ex-Senator, and two previous Captains of the R&A being croquet-style putters. They argued that it should be a permitted variation for those who may have physical problems that would not allow them to putt in a traditional style, questioned why the USGA should limit individual technique and stifle innovation, and cited the history and tradition of the croquet style of putting as well as the effect that this rules change would have on professionals and the club sales. However, in an unconscious echo of the R&A's debate over center-shafted clubs, the Executive Director, Joseph Dey, Jr., and the Executive Committee felt that they had to "preserve golf as golf" and "prevent it being modified into another game."

So, in 1968 the Rules of Golf prohibited straddling the line of putt. At the same time, a restriction was placed on the lie angle of the putter, requiring that the putter shaft diverge from the vertical by at least 10 degrees (Appendix II-1, d(i)). The latter of the two changes strikes me as a good way to handle the situation: rather than banning a technique or method, which then must be defined with potentially unforeseeable consequences, insert a simple specification that makes the improper technique impossible or at least very awkward. (The USGA later had to add a clarification that it was OK to straddle the line of a tap-in if doing so to avoid stepping in another player's line – an unforeseen complication.) Snead adapted by switching to a side-saddle style, standing beside the ball with both feet facing the hole and gripping the club as he had in the croquet style. He won two more Senior PGA Championships using this method of putting.

The side-saddle putting style helped golfers who had developed the "yips," but it called for an awkward stance that put a lot of strain on the back. For this reason, the long putter made its entrance into the game, enabling the player to gain the benefit of pivoting the putter off a fixed point (the anchored upper hand) without having to bend over as though tying his shoe.

We gave serious consideration to declaring the long putter to be nonconforming, using the "traditional and customary" clause as justification and the ban on croquet-style putting as precedent. The I&B committee discussed it in detail at a meeting in Atlanta in 1989, shortly after the Ping grooves lawsuit was filed, also shortly after Orville Moody's victory in the Senior Open with a long putter. Moody expressed his concern about rumors that the putter might be banned; so did club manufacturers, their "expression" including vague whispers about a possible lawsuit. With the sound of recent litigation still pinging in their ears, the Executive Committee decided to declare the long putter to be conforming, contrary to my recommendation. As this example demonstrates, an increasingly important political thread is the relationship between the USGA and the equipment makers.

In the early days, manufacturers of golf equipment were generally small businesses with a famous golfer or club maker as the founder or one of the partners. Their importance derived more from the quality of their workmanship than from their size. As mass production became possible and acceptable, the companies began to grow; the introduction of steel shafts and the use of forging machines (presses) for iron heads and carving machines for wood heads fueled their growth. (The carving machines had been originally designed to create wooden gunstocks and were adapted to the new purpose.)

In the mid 1960s, manufacturers generally introduced new club models every five years. There was very little difference in their products, since every club maker had the same factory equipment and the differences in club design were more aesthetic than performance-based. Golfers used to buy new clubs roughly every five years, so the manufacturers would change their models slightly to keep their happy customers from looking elsewhere.

As I said, this was the era when small, privately owned companies were dominant. Hogan, Hagen, Ram, Faultless, and Shakespeare were a few who were soon to merge with such larger companies as Spalding, Wilson, and MacGregor. Many of these larger companies had a complete line of golf products including balls. Acushnet, maker of Titleist, was one of a few ball-only companies. Few of the manufacturers were public companies, and meetings of the ball and club manufacturers' associations were friendly get-togethers because the market was healthy and growing. Marketing ideas were exchanged and even production processes were openly discussed, except for closely held secrets about ball production. This charade was amusing to watch as there were no secrets, because the same material suppliers, winding machine manufacturers, and mold makers serviced the entire industry.

In the mid 1960s, however, some new design concepts were introduced such as the less expensive solid-core two-piece ball, toe-heel weighting, and cavity-back clubs that were more forgiving than the standard blades, starting a new wave of competition.

Start-ups were entering the market with a single product and then expanding to other clubs. Examples of these are Ping (putter), Cleveland (woods and wedges), Cobra (bafflers, the utility wood), Callaway (Big Bertha), and TaylorMade (metal drivers). These companies have subsequently gone public or merged with bigger ones.

Large public companies now run the golf business, and the friendliness has gone the way of the persimmon driver and wound ball. The business has become cutthroat and the market has stopped growing. As a result, they feel the need to innovate more rapidly and get their new products in front of the consumer before the competitors can get to market, in some case introducing a new model up to three times a year – in many cases with very little measureable change in performance.

Where club pros used to be the main retailers, selling sets to their members, the market shifted to large chains of sporting goods or golf specialty stores that buy in bulk and offer lower prices. Component parts manufacturers who supply amateur club makers (numbering in the tens of thousands) have become a force as well. As the business concentrated into fewer hands and the financial consequences of unanticipated change became significant, the concomitant litigation problems became a fact of life for the ruling bodies. It behooves them to be in close communication with and take seriously the input of the manufacturers and their associations as they develop standards and consider new rules or changes. A logical sequence of events can make the transition to a rules change uneventful and relatively seamless.

When a problem – real or not – surfaces from whatever source, be it anecdotal or perceptual, it is important to define it clearly and quantify its magnitude by gathering all the evidence available. Is any action really needed? This question must be resolved before even considering any proposed change.

If the foregoing has been satisfied, make the evidence available to everyone who might be affected by the change, for consideration and comment. This includes but is not limited to golfers at large, administrators, associations, and the industry. If everybody can see the proven reason for a change and understand the effect on the game as a whole, the transition will be relatively smooth.

This kind of transparency is essential, and has been missing in the process recently.

Today, it seems that once a standard is proposed it is a done deal. Some input from the manufacturers have altered the numbers and even the implementation date, but not the overall concept and standard itself. This was not true in the past. Feedback from golfers played a vital role in addressing the ban on steel shafts in 1924 and the adoption of a lighter ball in 1930, which was repealed later that year.

To avoid the appearance of an autocratic process, the governors in 1976 included a "notice and comment" period so interested parties could present their views. This was effective during the adoption of the ODS in 1976 and also with the adoption of the symmetry rule for balls in 1980 and the reorganization of the rules and numerous changes in 1983. We had discussions with those who were most affected by the changes – explanatory, informative, and in most cases very amiable.

The process started falling apart in 1998 with the adoption of the limit on Coefficient of Restitution for clubs. Our instructions were to not say much but rather to listen, the implication being that we should filter all input by considering the speaker's hidden (or obvious) agenda. As a result, the USGA gets to hear about where it has made mistakes but doesn't take the opportunity to explain itself or to persuade either the manufacturers or the golfing public. The notice and comment process is sound and essential in good governance, but if the proposal presented is going to be adopted anyway, then why go through the process just for slight alterations?

In the COR example, the Executive Committee never made a formal proposal about adopting a standard. (I'm sorry if it seems that I keep harping on the COR situation, but it's the best example of how the process can break down and has had the most far-reaching implications of any equipment-rules decision since the acceptance of the Haskell ball.) The manufacturers knew that their clubs had a springlike effect after the USGA told them and gave them test data. I tried to persuade the committee to enforce the rule as written – *no springlike effect* – but to provide a generous grace period in which the average golfer could keep using such clubs, because the manufacturers had not violated the rule intentionally and we hadn't noticed it right away either. This was rejected, because it was viewed as potentially leading to another lawsuit. Rather than inviting the manufacturers into the process, the USGA viewed them as a potential adversary, one it was unwilling to fight. A century of concern about the ball going too far was trumped by fear of the consequences of regulating clubs that would propel the ball farther than ever.

As bad as this stance was, the R&A's position may have been worse. That body did not want to set any COR standard at all, preferring a delay tactic that had frequently worked in the past – "We are not sure of the extent of the problem and it will eventually work itself out so we don't have to deal with it now." This lack of action emboldened manufacturers to take advantage of the situation and make clubs for the world market with a COR of .860+ that exceeded the USGA .830 limit.

That was the state of things in early 2002 when the chairman of the USGA's I&B committee set out to achieve worldwide uniformity in the COR rules at last. He negotiated the following proposal with the R&A: The R&A would adopt a COR standard of .860, which was close to the maximum for most of the drivers in its jurisdiction; it would give golfers a grace period of six years, until January 2008, to use their clubs in everyday play but would adopt the USGA's .830

standard for its championships beginning in January 2003. The USGA would raise its own standard to .860 for nonchampionship play, beginning in 2003, while keeping the .830 limit for elite golfers in its championships – and then in 2008, both organizations would pull all clubs back to the .830 level. The end result would be a uniform standard worldwide, but the road to it would be a chaotic mess.

This proposal would have accomplished two remarkable things: It would have given the average American golfer the chance to buy a new, "hotter" club with the understanding that it would be illegal in six years; and it would have put a formal bifurcation of equipment standards into the rules for the first time. It would have done so at nearly the exact moment that the USGA and R&A were adopting a Joint Statement of Principles expressing their opposition to bifurcation of the rules. It was not the I&B chairman's finest hour.

Fortunately, those who reviewed the proposal reacted as one would hope. It was withdrawn, and the R&A did finally adopt the .830 standard for 2008 for the average golfer. I have no hard information regarding how many golfers under the R&A's jurisdiction have given up their .860 clubs. We hope golfers will be honorable, but we also hope the governing bodies will exercise some common sense in making the rules.

In 2002, after fifteen years of argument and persuasion about the need for such a document, the USGA and R&A decided, to adopt a joint Statement of Principles (SOP), a uniform code that would put forward the philosophical basis for equipment rules and the intentions against which they should be judged. (See Appendix I for the full Statement of Principles.)

The SOP amounts to a codification of the song that USGA presidents and the executive committee have been singing for a hundred years. It states that golfers at the highest level are hitting the ball as far as we want them to and if that distance should ever increase – "from advancing equipment technology, greater athleticism of players, improved player coaching, golf course conditioning or a combination of these or other factors" – the organizations would have to consider taking steps to protect the challenge of the game.

The organizations acknowledge in the SOP that golf balls have reached but not exceeded the initial velocity and overall distance limits established in the Rules and add that they "are not advocating that the Rules relating to golf ball specifications be changed other than to modernize test methods." However, they immediately go on to lay out the dire consequences to the game if distance should increase, even if that increase had nothing to do with equipment but grew out of improved athleticism, technique, or course conditioning: "The consequential lengthening or toughening of courses would be costly or impossible and would have a negative effect on increasingly important environmental and ecological issues. Pace of play would be slowed and playing costs would increase."

I do wonder sometimes about the world inhabited by those who govern the game, as opposed to all those who play it. I have not noticed in my experience that the game has gotten too easy; I don't think that too many people reading these words have found that to be the case, either. The ruling bodies spend too much time focusing on the exploits of the very best golfers, the elite 0.001% who play in their championships. They don't seem to worry much about the effect their rulings will have on the vast majority of players, those dogged victims who love golf dearly and have kept it alive for hundreds of years. For most of us, it makes no difference if the back tees are set at 7,000 yards or 7,200 or 8,000, because we aren't playing from them anyway (or shouldn't be). If a course or club feels obliged to spend heavily to stretch the course to accommodate the one or two percent of golfers who don't feel challenged from the back tees already, it's not allocating its resources with much good judgment. The trend over the last thirty years has been to make courses more difficult, by ringing greens with bunkers and introducing water features that penalize the weaker golfer but look lovely in the brochure. According to the USGA's Slope System, a Slope of 113 represents a course of "standard difficulty." How many courses have you seen with Slope ratings below 113?

And in the midst of all this, the USGA and R&A have consistently made rulings that make the game more difficult for the average golfer, in the interests of "protecting the game" from the efforts of the very best.

The wisdom of the ruling bodies should be judged by the health of the game. Golf is not attracting new players, even as it tries to gain footholds in untapped parts of the world. It's too expensive, takes too long, and is one of the hardest sports to learn, especially at the beginning. It needs ways to entice people to stay in the game, not rules that make it tougher for them.

An important paragraph in the SOP reads, "The R&A and the USGA continue to believe that the retention of a single set of rules for all players of the game, irrespective of ability, is one of golf's greatest strengths. The R&A and the USGA regard the prospect of having permanent separate rules for elite competition as undesirable and have no current plans to create separate equipment rules for highly skilled players."

The dirty word lurking behind this passage is *bifurcation*: dividing the Rules of Golf in two. I was responsible for initiating all the equipment rules changes over a period of twenty-six years, mostly in collaboration with a colleague from the R&A. It was the time when advanced technology and science started playing a significant role in equipment design and regulation. While with the USGA, certainly over the first twenty years or so, I was totally in agreement with the notion that the game was one for all and that having a uniform set of rules was paramount. I believed that a single set of rules was the most important element in the essence of the game and the very matrix binding integrity to the game.

During the final years of my tenure and soon after leaving, I found myself questioning this principle, not because it didn't make sense but rather because the game itself was splitting in two. The uniform set of rules was increasingly becoming ineffective. We were seeing bifurcation through application.

There has always been a difference between serious and casual golf when it comes to the rules. Golfers have long created their own version of "local rules," the locality consisting of their own fourball. Some of these include playing a mulligan, treating out-of-bounds as a lateral hazard, getting or asking for advice, rolling the ball in the fairway (winter rules in July), dropping a ball where you think you lost it instead of applying stroke-and-distance, a player off the green goes first even if he's closer to the hole – the list goes on and on. They do it for numerous reasons: ignorance, perhaps; unwillingness to conform to a very strict code; a desire to keep things moving; belief that the rules didn't apply to their particular circumstances. Once a single rule is violated, it becomes easy to throw in a few more that are questionable and even some which are merely inconvenient.

I believe golf is golf, be it on a Sunday evening when playing by yourself, a match with a couple of good friends, or a club championship. The Rules set the conditions under which we can judge our performance against others and, most important, against ourselves. This comforting axiom has become harder to maintain, not because the majority of American golfers have a propensity toward self-determination, but because participants have evolved into two distinct and disproportionately sized skill groups. This is clearly acknowledged by the game's guardians, who are so heavily influenced by the very visible elite golfers and well recognized by the majority who don't believe that some of the rules promulgated by the guardians are appropriate. I'm not referring to the casual disregards I mentioned above, like mulligans, but rather minute restrictions on equipment that limit the ways it can help make the game more enjoyable for the nonchampionship golfer. If rules don't make sense, the majority will ignore them; the average golfer realized there was no good reason to bar distance-measuring devices long before the ruling bodies caught on.

The dilemma for the guardians is how to develop a code that effectively spans the gap between the elite and the masses (95% of the participants), while protecting the challenge the game has to offer. If the code – to which the majority of participants are expected to adhere voluntarily – does not make intuitive sense and is inappropriate for the context of their play, they will defect, and such actions undermine the authority of the ruling organizations. When people believe their leaders are deaf to their concerns, they rebel or withdraw or find new leaders.

The USGA and R&A have too often based their decisions on the performance of the extraordinary, and building a code for all based on the performance of a very few is nearly impossible.

Golf is such a wonderful and addictive activity, and playing by the rules not only lends order to the game but enhances one's appreciation of its traditions and rich history. The more that people play by the rules the healthier it will become and the more it will grow, while its essential integrity remains intact.

Because of the insoluble dilemma facing the guardians, I have reconsidered my position about an across-the-board uniform set of rules. For most people, the playing rules as described in "A Quick Guide to the Rules of Golf" presented on the R&A website (which can be downloaded for free) or "The Rules in Brief" on the USGA website (which can be purchased for 75 cents) will be sufficient to cover nearly all the circumstances they are likely to encounter. These do need to be understandably expanded for serious competition – we cannot and should not scrap the whole of the Rules of Golf –to ensure that unlikely situations are covered in advance. But for the vast majority of us, these truncated rules publications above will serve, perhaps augmented with the essential principles of Play it as it Lays, Take the Course as You Find it, and Keep the Game Moving.

There is no need to tamper with the equipment rules or make them more restrictive unless the introduction of such equipment is detrimentally affecting the challenge experienced by the majority of golfers. If there is a consensus backed by evidence that some equipment affects the essences of the game at the elite level, then a local rule or condition of competition can effectively be adopted for these events. This is the lesser of two evils – one being the adoption of new rules only because a very small group *may* be causing a problem, and the other being a defection from voluntary adherence, which will undermine the authority of the governors. The alterations to the groove specifications in Appendix II-5(c) for 2010 provide an example of this kind of de facto bifurcation, as the change applies immediately for the elites but not until 2024 for the masses. The so-called One Ball Rule is another example that the pros must follow, while the rest of us can roll our own.

These types of practical adjustments are a deviation from the Statement of Principles, but provide a solution to the guardians' dilemma. They do not require a formal bifurcation of the rules, merely the recognition that a simplified version of the playing and equipment rules is good enough for most play, while the rest can be covered through Conditions of Competition. This approach should result in a stronger following and respect for the rules, which in turn will give the guardians the authority they deserve.

This will be good for the game and will help move the world of golf in the direction of peace.

CHAPTER FIVE

# A Clear Path Forward

"You may as well praise a man for not robbing a bank." It's one of the most famous quotes in golf, and it reflects something good and precious in the game that's been slipping away from us, something we need to restore as much as we can. In the first round of the 1925 U.S. Open, Bobby Jones's ball was in long grass beside the eleventh green of the Worcester Country Club. As he prepared to hit his shot, he saw the ball settle slightly into the grass. Though no observers believed he had caused the ball's movement, he promptly called a one-stroke penalty on himself and ignored USGA officials who told him this was unnecessary. The incident contributed to an opening 77; he ultimately lost the championship in a playoff with Willie Macfarlane. Take away the penalty stroke and there would be no playoff, and Jones would have five U.S. Open wins, an unequalled total.

He dismissed after-the-fact comments on his honesty and sportsmanship with the quote above. Less remembered is the second sentence he put with it: "There is only one way to play the game."

Golf, unique among sports, has always been a game of honor. Its roots are in match play, one against one, but in its truest form it is one against oneself. It is the most beguiling method of testing and measuring ourselves that man has ever devised, and even in its competitions it needs no umpire or referee to stand over the participants and ensure their compliance with the rules. (Officials are provided to answer questions when needed, but that's a very different thing than having someone blow a whistle or throw a flag when your ball moves at address.)

I don't think it's naïve to bring this attitude into the area of equipment regulation.

Golfers on every level of the game want to play fair. The USGA and the R&A have no police force, no Swiss Guards, no way to compel obedience except in their own championships. The professional tours choose to follow their regulations, but there's nothing to stop them from doing otherwise. If the PGA Tour decided to eliminate all restrictions on balls and clubs or institute a three-stroke penalty for hitting a ball into a hazard, the USGA could shake its collective head but that's all. If your weekend foursome wants to declare all out-of-bounds to be treated as a lateral hazard you can do so, though such rounds cannot be used for an official USGA handicap, if you care about that. (And if you want to submit them anyway, nobody else is going to know.)

When Callaway brought out the nonconforming ERC II in 2001, with a COR greater than the USGA limit, it learned that the average golfer did not want to use a club perceived as giving an unfair advantage -- even if Arnold Palmer endorsed it, as he did the ERC II. When the groove specifications were changed as a condition of competition on the PGA Tour in 2010, the USGA provided a tester who traveled with the pros in case someone wanted to be certain his clubs were conforming; the tester discovered he had less to do than anticipated because nearly all pros had already checked and tested their clubs in advance or the manufacturers had done this for them. Similar precautions had proven unnecessary with the COR limit on Tour, noted Dick Rugge, the USGA's senior technical director. "[The portable testing device] became a dust collector," Rugge told *Golfweek*. "It [was used] once a month, then once every four months, then once every year, and then the Tour said, 'We're not going to bring it out here.' They don't even have one anymore."

After five hundred years of playing the game and a hundred of governing it so its implements remain "traditional and customary," we've reached a point where the rules and regulations are pretty well established and the performance differences are truly minuscule. The simple fact that we can measure a characteristic does not mean that measurable violations lead to enhanced performance results.

This last point is something the manufacturers don't want us to realize. When one club maker advertises its driver as having "the highest MOI [moment of inertia] of any club," it hopes you'll assume that means it's the best there is. But does "the highest MOI" mean it performs differently from the second-highest MOI, or the tenth, or the hundredth? Not to any degree that will make even one stroke's difference in your score.

There was a great hue and cry a few years ago when Nike had to pull its Sumo2 driver from the shelves because some were found to exceed the COR limit. It shouldn't have been a surprise to anybody; when you engineer a club to incorporate the manufacturing tolerance of any limit, you will likely run into the variations (up and down) that are the reason for the tolerance in the first place. Nike Golf president Bob Wood acknowledged as much, referring to the Characteristic Time (CT) test that supplemented the COR standard, "I don't think anybody can sell a driver made at 239 [microseconds, the actual CT limit that corresponds to a COR of .822, with a manufacturing tolerance of 18 microseconds bringing it up to a COR of .830]. I'd be pulling your leg if I didn't say that we didn't try to get as close as possible to the limit." He also said that the difference in distance was at most one or two yards; in fact, it's less than a yard.

I'm willing to say that such small differences don't matter, and the USGA shouldn't concern itself with the occasional accidental violation of its specifications. This differs from the situation in the Ping Eye2 lawsuit, because in that case – while the differences were tiny and the performance effect negligible – Karsten Manufacturing refused, for some time, to bring the clubs into compliance even after it was informed of the problem. No one won a tournament or shot a course record because they used Ping Eye2 grooves; that wasn't the issue. It was whether the USGA had the power to make regulations and make them stick in the face of outright defiance. (There was an amusing postscript twenty years later: You'll recall that as part of the final agreement between the USGA and Karsten, clubs manufactured before the agreement were deemed to be conforming regardless of future changes in groove specifications. When the new groove regulations were introduced and adopted as a condition of competition for 2010 on the PGA Tour, a few professionals went and found their old pre-1990 Ping Eye2 wedges and used them in tournaments. They no doubt felt they were getting away with something, but there was no noticeable difference in their results.)

Once again, intent points the way to sound regulation. If there is no intent to go beyond the specification, there's no need to concern yourself with detailed field inspections or punishing trivial, inadvertent violations. (I should note here that I'm only talking about small variations; large ones may matter and should not be tolerated. The horse that went out the barn door was composed of springlike effect; after that, everything else has been about how to better keep it shut, but nothing's going to bring her back.)

The laws of physics govern our golf game more thoroughly than the USGA or R&A ever could.

The USGA over a period of twenty years from 1975 to 1995 assembled an impressive group of highly skilled and qualified researchers, capable of understanding in the most intricate detail exactly how and why equipment performs the way it does. The R&A has finally joined the party in recent years and hired a well-qualified and skilled scientist on a full-time basis. These people are fully capable, if directed properly, of determining the effect that minor changes in equipment will have on human performance and when these become measureable and meaningful. Science should be used to help simplify the rules, recognizing where nature has drawn the lines on performance and where – when left to their own interpretative abilities – letting manufacturers and designers apply the intent of a rule will be more effective than trying to monitor any set of complex standards requiring sophisticated measuring devices and complicated field tests and reams of lists to find the exact model and markings on a particular club.

Before contemplating any new regulation, the rules makers must be certain there is a specific need for a change and be able to justify this to their constituents. The Rules of Golf have seen subtle shifts over the years, but the underlying principles are traditional and unchanging. In most cases, changes are made either to clarify the intent or interpretation of an existing rule or to solve a problem. If you're trying to solve a problem, the problem must be clearly and specifically defined; you can't effectively solve a problem if you can't precisely define it. Proposed solutions must carry some evidence that (1) there is a problem, and (2) they will solve it. (Sounds self-evident, but as we've seen too often, it's not.) If you can't do both of those things, then you need further experimentation to establish the existence of the problem and the effectiveness of the solution. It's especially important to think about the long-term effects, both on the ability to monitor and enforce the rule change and how it might change the game.

As long as science is being used to develop equipment, it must be used to understand how equipment works and also how to simplify the rules that control it. It is of utmost importance to understand the effect of equipment changes and how they affect performance in the hands of various golfers. If, for instance, a higher COR will increase the speed of the ball, we need to know by how much and whether this will affect the outcome of a competition or the challenge the game offers. Even when the effect is significant, there is no need for precise standards; intent provides the best guide. If springlike effect is going to affect performance significantly, then don't permit it; the rule should state, clearly, *the club shall not be designed or manufactured to have at impact the effect of a spring*. No precise measuring standard needs to be adopted, but it is important that the governors have the ability, using an internal test to see if the face is contributing to enhanced ball speed by design. This is using science the way it should be used, and if the manufacturers need to use the same test so be it. But a sophisticated technically complex standard invites challenge.

Some examples of how the intent rules work:

*The requirement that the shaft be straight.* (See Rules Appendix II-2. Shaft.) The regulation states that "[t]he shaft must be straight from the top of the grip to a point not more than 5 inches above the sole…" and that "[e]xcept for putters all of the heel portion of the club must lie within .625 inches of the plane containing the axis of the straight part of the shaft and the [intended] (horizontal) line of play." There are no specifications regarding "straightness," and we strongly resisted adopting such specs. Setting a limit implies that clubs or balls that are outside the permitted range somehow perform better. If they don't – and bent shafts wouldn't – then why waste time and effort measuring and testing? Just say no and stay out of the "specification black hole."

*The requirement that the shaft bend the same way no matter how it is rotated about its own axis, and twist the same way in both directions.* We revised this rule in 1984 because the previous rule requiring that the shaft be circular in cross-section was not effective and left out the intent of the rule. The rule now describes the intended physical properties of a shaft that is "circular in cross section." After the introduction of composite shafts (graphite), it was possible to design a shaft that was circular in cross section but had different bending properties depending on the axis about which it was bent and could also have different twisting properties depending on the angle of the fiber wrap. We had two choices: We could try to quantify the differences in degrees of twist or deflection of bend under a precise load, at a given specified length of lever arm, and at certain loads, etc., etc., etc., or we could say it must be designed to twist and bend the same way no matter how we bend or twist it about its own axis. It was an easy decision.

*The requirement that the ball perform as if it were spherically symmetrical.* A ball is intended to have symmetrical performance properties. It was never so stated, but this is certainly everyone's general understanding of what constitutes a "ball." As we saw in the example of the Polara ball, the game's challenge would be compromised if an aerodynamic design allowed the ball itself to correct a slice or hook or other swing flaw. To make the violation clear, we immediately adopted a specification and test to measure flight trajectory height, distance, and time in flight when the ball was launched spinning about different axes. If the differences in these measurements were outside certain limits, the ball would be considered nonconforming (asymmetrical). Unfortunately, there were some balls that were caught by this test not because of any intentional asymmetrical design but because of manufacturing tolerances or an intentional flat spot where the brand or model was stamped. When we told the affected manufacturers about the problem they immediately modified their designs and fell back into the conforming range.

This particular exercise showed us that the standard was overly restrictive; slight deviations made no real performance difference, and there was no intent on the part of the manufacturer to make asymmetric balls. In 1996 we took out the specifications and emphasized intent instead. The USGA is perfectly capable of measuring a ball's symmetrical properties very accurately, but it would wisely prefer to warn a manufacturer of any deviation that approaches the guiding limits – small deviations don't really matter – and the manufacturer is usually grateful. No lists, no routine lengthy and cumbersome test protocols, just a rule based on intent, backed by science and enforced accordingly.

Is it a matter of life or death if someone unintentionally violates an equipment rule? Does a violation mean the difference between winning or losing? How can there be any effective adherence to the rule by the participants if it is too complicated to comprehend or difficult to apply? Instead of having a complicated rule, it would surely be more effective to have a simple rule whose intent is clear, and if in doubt to let an official make the decision on the spot, with no penalty to the player if there is a subsequent decision that the product doesn't conform.

Consider the list of conforming drivers. Such a list – and now, a similar list for irons on account of their groove configurations – is very cumbersome and costly to produce. It is difficult to maintain and keep updated; revisions are made every Monday by 12:00 noon, and it must be 100% correct and contain every club submitted for the last fifteen years or more. This list is best used in only those few championships where notice is posted of a condition of competition; at local events it is extremely time-consuming to use and enforce. Most important, the difference between a club that conforms and one that doesn't will have a negligible effect on performance in the hands of a golfer no matter how good he/she may be.

With the above in mind, here's my question: Is it really worth it to regulate equipment as we do? How can this degree of complexity be good for the game?

If the intent of any specific rule is made clear – as clear as possible to golfers and manufacturers – the golfer will have a better chance of enforcing it for himself. It is ultimately his responsibility to follow the rules, to use equipment that conforms. As far as the manufacturer is concerned, if the intent of the specification within the rules is clear, he can design and manufacture a product with the intention of meeting those specifications. If he elects not to do so after being warned that his product is in violation, then is the time to make it well known that his product doesn't conform with the Rules of Golf.

The USGA should develop specifications based on its research into which properties in equipment really make a difference. If the research shows a particular standard is necessary, the USGA could prevent any misunderstanding on the part of manufacturers by making the intent of the rule crystal clear and perhaps provide help in making measurements. It should both notify the manufacturers and publish the results on its website, along with the standard to control it. Only when manufacturers are in doubt about the standard or how their club compares to it would they need to submit a sample.

This is the case now with balls and clubs, most of which are not submitted, and in the past never had to be submitted as long as they were manufactured to conform with the rules. Unfortunately, the USGA has created its own burden of testing by adopting some standards that are so complex and have so little to do with real performance that compliance can only be monitored by maintaining an ongoing list of conforming clubs.

The USGA should develop an identifiable emblem – perhaps the organization's seal, or something with the letters USGA – that is licensed to manufacturers as an indication that their products conform with the Rules of Golf, to be featured on the equipment and its packaging and in advertising. The USGA can check such products periodically or whenever there is some indication that an item may be nonconforming; there are no secrets among manufacturers or professionals when a potential competitive advantage is at stake, and if something funny's going on, the USGA will hear about it. This would be significantly less work than what it is doing right now and more successful than building a "specification and compliance" black hole.

The words "Conforms with the Rules of Golf" are a powerful endorsement, and a visible indication that the product conforms would be a strong incentive for the manufacturers to abide by the USGA's standards. The USGA imprimatur would be the equivalent of the "*Good Housekeeping* Seal of Approval," and as we saw with Callaway and the ERC II, golfers on all levels do want to use conforming clubs.

It is not a matter of life and death if a slight mishap in production causes some clubs to fall outside the standard. If there are such violations, the manufacturer would be asked to bring its equipment back to within manufacturing tolerances; if this is done, then all is well. If the manufacturer refuses or fails to make a good faith effort to correct the problem, then the USGA's license will be withdrawn *for all products made by that manufacturer* for a period of three years. The manufacturers would have to agree to this in advance, as a condition of the process of applying for the license.

From the player's point of view, if it says on the club or on the packaging that the item conforms, then it is OK to use. If the club does not include a statement of conformity, the player should consult the USGA/R&A if in doubt, as stated in the preamble of our current rules. If the rule is an intent rule, the player will be better able to judge conformity than if the club requires a rigorous, technically sophisticated test. You don't really need a microscope and calipers to determine if a shaft is straight; for all intents and purposes, it will be pretty obvious to the player. If his new putter has a prism of sighting windows, he should be suspicious with regard to the "plain in shape" rule. He won't have to go to a cumbersome listing of clubs, but rather just look for a conformation statement on the club. There may be some problems in monitoring this procedure, but those problems are mild when compared to the present process. This is where the USGA should be spending its money – monitoring equipment and working with the manufacturers, not making the process more complex for the player and official. There are exceptions that should be carefully addressed, but the mission to simplify is pure and worthy of complete consideration without bias.

If a question arises at an event about a product's conforming status, an official should have the option to give the player the benefit of the doubt and ask him to check with the USGA before using it again. Or the official, based on his interpretation of the rule, may suggest that the piece of equipment not be used until the USGA has been consulted. This procedure has some minor pitfalls, but it is important to remember that slight violations of these rules of intent make no measureable difference in performance and certainly will not be the difference between winning and losing a match or tournament. The simplicity and overall effectiveness far outweigh the problems created by an increasing array of detailed technical specifications.

In a game of honor, there's no place for using the rules to say, "Gotcha!" Players and manufacturers should not be punished for good-faith or unintentional violations; penalty provisions will only come into play if the offenses are egregious and repeated. If a player uses a piece of equipment after he has been informed that it is nonconforming, he will be disqualified. If a manufacturer refuses to bring its equipment in line with established guidelines, it will have its Statement of Conformity revoked and this fact will be made public. This is all the punishment our game needs.

For all of our sophisticated testing, it wasn't the USGA that found springlike effect in titanium drivers; it was a phone call from a manufacturer's competitor that tipped us off. Masters officials used to send us balls they recovered from Rae's Creek and other water hazards to see if they were conforming or not. The tournament circuit is the greatest test range anyone could ask for; if someone is getting an extra edge by using something fishy, we'll hear about it one way or another. The competitive market is very efficient that way.

In the meantime, the USGA will continue to test equipment for manufacturers and develop research methods to improve test procedures. It will also conduct research to determine how changes in the properties of equipment can affect the game. The technical department of the USGA is a strong and vital part of the organization. With easier-to-understand rules based on intent, we can come closer to the ideal use of science and technology to support and bolster the game and can move forward into the second half of our game's millennium with regulations based on knowledge and principles rather than fear of the unknown.

## APPENDIX I

# Joint Statement of Principles

*Complete text of Joint Statement of Principles, adopted by the USGA and the R&A in 2002.*

As the governing authorities for the Rules of Golf including equipment Rules, The R&A in St. Andrews, Scotland and the United States Golf Association (USGA) have continued to monitor closely the effects of advancing equipment technology on the playing of the game. The R&A and the USGA are also aware that this subject has attracted wide-ranging comment and a number of conflicting views.

History has proved that it is impossible to foresee the developments in golf equipment that advancing technology will deliver. It is of the greatest importance to golf's continuing appeal that such advances are judged against a clear and broadly accepted series of principles.

The purpose of this statement is to set out the joint views of the R&A and the USGA, together with the framework of key principles and policies which guide their actions.

In a historical context, the game has seen progressive developments in the clubs and balls available to golfers who, through almost six centuries, have sought to improve their playing performance and enjoyment.

While generally welcoming this progress, the R&A and the USGA will remain vigilant when considering equipment Rules. The purpose of the Rules is to protect golf's best traditions, to prevent an over-reliance on technological advances rather than skill, and to ensure that skill is the dominant element of success throughout the game.

The R&A and the USGA continue to believe that the retention of a single set of rules for all players of the game, irrespective of ability, is one of golf's greatest strengths. The R&A and the USGA regard the prospect of having permanent separate rules for elite competition as undesirable and have no current plans to create separate equipment rules for highly skilled players.

Golf balls used by the vast majority of highly skilled players today have largely reached the performance limits for initial velocity and overall distance which have been part of the Rules since 1976. The governing bodies believe that golf balls, when hit by highly skilled golfers, should not of themselves fly significantly further than they do today. In the current circumstances, the R&A and the USGA are not advocating that the Rules relating to golf ball specifications be changed other than to modernize test methods.

The R&A and the USGA believe, however, that any further significant increases in hitting distances at the highest level are undesirable. Whether these increases in distance emanate from advancing equipment technology, greater athleticism of players, improved player coaching, golf course conditioning or a combination of these or other factors, they will have the impact of seriously reducing the challenge of the game. The consequential lengthening or toughening of courses would be costly or impossible and would have a negative effect on increasingly important environmental and ecological issues. Pace of play would be slowed and playing costs would increase.

The R&A and the USGA will consider all of these factors contributing to distance on a regular basis. Should such a situation of meaningful increases in distances arise, the R&A and the USGA would feel it immediately necessary to seek ways of protecting the game.

In determining any future amendments to the Rules, or to

associated procedures that may from time to time prove necessary, the R&A and the USGA will continue their respective policies of consultation with interested parties, including the use of notice and comment procedures, and will take account of the views expressed. The achievement and maintenance of worldwide uniformity in equipment rules through close coordination between the R&A and the USGA is a clear priority.

The R&A and the USGA are concerned that, on an increasing number of occasions, new products are being developed and marketed which potentially run counter to the principles expressed in this statement. These product launches, without prior consultation with the governing bodies, can lead to considerable difficulties in formulating appropriate equipment rules and to undesirable conflicts between manufacturers and rule makers. The R&A and the USGA intend to bring forward proposals designed to improve procedures for the approval of new products.

The R&A and the USGA believe that the principles stated in this document will, when carefully applied, serve the best interests of the game of golf.

.

# APPENDIX II

# Timeline of Golf Equipment and Rules

**1452**    First recorded sale of a golf ball, for 10 shillings. Balls were primarily made of beech and boxwood.

**1457**    The Scottish Parliament, under King James II of Scotland, bans golf and futball (soccer) and encourages the practice of archery. This was the first of three times that the Scottish Parliament banned "gowf."

**1500**    Featherie invented. This new type of ball was made from bull-hide stuffed with wet feathers. It traveled farther than wooden balls, up to 150 yards on a good drive.

**1502**    King James IV makes the first recorded purchase of golf equipment, a set of clubs from a bowmaker in Perth, Scotland.

**1554**    The record books of the Town Council of Edinburgh reference the golf ball makers of Leith, with indications that these early golf balls were made of leather.

**1603**    William Mayne is appointed by King James VI (James I of England) as his personal club maker.

**1618**    King James VI of Scotland declares an embargo on importing featheries and grants a twenty-one year monopoly on ball-making to James Melvill of St. Andrews. *(There is no evidence that this license stopped anyone else from becoming a ball maker, nor is there any evidence that Melvill was one himself.)*

**1636**    The first documented reference to iron clubs, as well as clubs designed specifically for playing from a bunker, appears in a Latin grammar written in Aberdeen, Scotland. Document also contains the earliest known reference to teeing a ball, as well as the first direct reference to a "hole."

**1642**    John Dickson receives a license as ball maker for Aberdeen, Scotland.

**1687**    The diary of Thomas Kincaid, a doctor from Edinburgh, contains the first references on how golf clubs are made.

**1691**    A letter written by Professor Alexander Munro, a Regent at the University of St. Andrews, contains the reference to a "set" of golf clubs comprising a "play club, scraper, and tin faced club."

**1729**    An inventory of the estate of William Burnet, Governor of Massachusetts, includes a reference to golf clubs and may be identified as the earliest reference to golf in America.

**1743**    Thomas Mathison's epic *The Goff, An Heroi-Comical Poem in Three Cantos*, is the first publication devoted solely to golf. It contains the first detailed description of the manufacture of a feathery ball.

Customs accounts document a shipment of ninety-six golf clubs and 432 golf balls from Leith, Scotland to Charleston, South Carolina.

**1744**    First documented code of Rules of Golf by the Gentlemen Golfers of Leith (later known as the Honourable Company of Edinburgh Golfers).

**1748**    Documentary evidence of a shipment of golf clubs and golf balls from Scotland to Russia.

**1750** Customs accounts document shipments of golf clubs and golf balls from Greenock, Scotland, to Virginia.

**1765** Customs accounts document shipments of golf clubs and golf balls from Glasgow and West Lothian to Maryland and North Carolina.

**1779** *Rivington's Royal Gazette*, published in New York, contains a notice advertising the sale of golf clubs and golf balls.

**1803** A record book from the Honourable Company of Edinburgh Golfers contains the first known reference to an iron club designed specifically for putting; earlier references to putters all describe wooden-headed clubs.

**1812** Hugh Philp, sometimes known as the "Stradivarius of Golf," opens a club repair and refurbishing business in St. Andrews.

**1828** Hickory imported from America is used to make golf shafts.

**1836** The longest drive ever recorded with a featherie ball, 361 yards, is achieved by Samuel Messieux on the Elysian Fields on the Old Course at St. Andrews.

**1845** Gutta percha ball invented by Rob Paterson. Ball is fashioned from tree gum rounded into shape. Originally smooth, later versions were scuffed and hammered to enhance performance. They were approximately 1.7 inches in diameter and light for their size (1.35 to 1.55 ounces).

**1881** A mold is used for cover patterns on gutta-perchas. Golfers had found that the guttie flew much truer after it had been hit several times and scuffed up slightly.

**1887**    P.G. Tait, Professor of Natural Philosophy at the University of Edinburgh, begins publishing scientific papers on the science of golf, including spin, ball flight properties, trajectories, and wind effects.

**1894**    A.G. Spalding offers for sale the first golf clubs made in America.

       USGA established.

**1895**    The pool cue is banned as a putter by the USGA.

**1897**    R&A's Rules of Golf Committee is formed.

**1898**    Haskell ball invented by Bert Work and Coburn Haskell. The ball consisted of rubber thread wound under tension around a central core of relatively nonelastic material, and encased in a gutta or balata shell.

**1899**    Dr. George Grant, one of the first African-Americans to graduate from Harvard College, receives the first patent for a wooden golf tee, but he never markets the product commercially.

**1900**    Haskell ball used in team matches on Long Island between British and American collegians. The British competitors derided it with the name "bounding billy" and felt it was unsporting.

       John Gammeter develops a thread-winding machine that allows for the mass production of the new rubber-core golf ball.

**1901**    Walter Travis wins his second U.S. Amateur, becoming the first golfer to win a major title with a rubber-cored golf ball.

**1902** E. Burr of England receives a patent for "rib-faced" irons with exaggerated grooves to impart additional spin on the golf ball.

**1903** Arthur Franklin Knight patents the controversial "Schenectady" center-shafted mallet putter.

**1904** Walter Travis wins the British Amateur using a Schenectady center-shafted putter.

**1907** The USGA considers the possibility of standardizing the golf ball to control its resiliency and liveliness, fearing the need for courses to stretch to extraordinary lengths.

**1908** First appearance in R&A Rules of statement on Form and Make of Golf Clubs.

William Taylor introduces dimples on golf balls.

Frank Mingay patents a golf ball with a liquid center in an elastic shell.

**1909** USGA includes Form and Make clause in its rules, using the R&A's wording.

**1910** R&A bans all center-shafted clubs "of the mallet-headed type, or such clubs as have a neck so bent as to achieve the same effect."

The first patent for a steel shaft is issued to Arthur F. Knight of Schenectady, N.Y.

**1911** The USGA puts the R&A language regarding mallet-headed clubs into its Form and Make clause, but adds, "The shaft of a putter may be fixed at the heel or at any other point in the head. The term mallet headed, as above used, when applied to putters does not embrace putters of the so-called Schenectady type. " This marks the beginning of a forty-two-year period with two official versions of the Rules of Golf.

**1913**  Spalding introduces balls in different sizes: large, medium and small. The arrangement of their dimples varies as well.

**1915**  Patent expires on Haskell ball, which increased competition. In a quest for the most efficient combination of size and weight over the years, manufacturers have generally settled on 1.62 ounces and 1.63 inches as the most efficient.

Spalding catalog lists compression, which ranged from 8 to 4.25; the lower the number, the harder the ball.

**1920**  USGA and R&A agree on a clause titled "The Limitation of Ball," which states: "The weight of the ball shall not be greater than 1.62 ounces avoirdupois and the size not less than 1.62 inches in diameter. The Rules of Golf Committee and the Executive Committee of the USGA will take whatever steps they think necessary to limit the power of the ball with regard to distance, should any ball of greater power be introduced."

This rule went into effect in 1921.

Swingweight scale developed, based on the balance of Francis Ouimet's clubs.

**1921**  William Lowell invents the Reddy Tee, a wooden peg shaped on top to hold a ball, to be pushed into the ground. He pays Walter Hagen and trick-shot artist Joe Kirkwood to promote the invention, which catches on. A patent for this invention was issued in 1926.

The R&A bans clubs with corrugated, grooved or slotted faces.

**1922** Note is added to the Form and Make of Golf Clubs section of the USGA Rules: "A steel shaft club is a departure from the traditional and accepted form of golf clubs." Walter Hagen wins the Open Championship (British), the first native-born American citizen to win the title. Later in the year, he becomes the first golf professional to establish a golf equipment company using his own name.

**1923** USGA Executive Committee refuses to approve the steel shaft, but it agrees to try them out. It asks amateurs to try them and report back to the committee. Results showed little difference in performance between hickory and steel.

USGA adopts restrictions on clubface markings: "Effective January 1, 1924, the club faces shall not bear any lines, dots, or other markings made for the obvious purpose of putting a cut on the ball, nor shall they be stamped or cut with lines exceeding 1/16 inch in width, nor less than 3/32 inch apart, measured on their inside edges. Both line and dot markings may be used, either alone or in combination within the above limitations, provided all rough or raised edges are removed."

**1924** Executive Committee of the USGA declared steel shafts conforming and permitted in all competitions. R&A does not adopt steel shafts at this time.

**1925** Official statement included in USGA Rules: "Steel shaft clubs as at present manufactured may be used in competitions."

Royal Canadian Golf Association decides to allow steel shafts, despite the R&A position that they are nonconforming.

USGA and R&A hold discussions to attempt to decide upon a standard golf ball by regulating size and weight.

The USGA's Implements and Ball Committee believe a ball not less than 1.68 inches in diameter nor more than 1.55 ounces in weight will meet the requirements of all types of players. The R&A wants a unified standard, so the final decision is postponed to January 1926.

**1926** The R&A and USGA decide not to adopt a new standard ball because the majority of golfers have not had a chance to test it out. The USGA expressed the view that "it would be a great mistake for the USGA to adopt a standard ball unless this action was supported by the golfing fraternity at large, and no action shall be taken until such support is assured." For trial purposes, the USGA asks manufacturers to make limited quantities of the 1.68/1.55 ball; manufacturers were asked to submit their views on the proposed change to the ball, which is being considered in an effort to control the distance of the ball.

The first fairway irrigation system is installed at Brook Hollow Country Club in Dallas, Texas.

The USGA and R&A agree to ban deep-grooved irons.

**1927** The Rules of Golf Committees of the USGA & R&A agree on the following points:

1. Regulation of the driving power of the ball is greatly needed.

2. No change in the ball should result in less pleasurable playing qualities.

3. Any change in the ball should be adopted simultaneously and be identical in both the U.S. and the U.K.

4. If, in addition to a specification covering size and weight, a simple and dependable method of measuring

resilience can be devised, complete control of the driving power of the ball seems possible.

A resilience test machine is designed by Professor Harold Thomas of Carnegie Institute in Pittsburgh.

**1928**  Specific measurements for markings on clubfaces removed from rule book; new rule addresses intent only, barring markings "for the obvious purpose of putting a cut on the ball." Shallow line and dot markings may be used.

Professor Thomas's ball resiliency machine is mechanically simplified and produces dependable data. William C. Fownes, Jr., past president of the USGA, makes arrangements to manufacture eight of these machines, including one for the R&A and others available for golf ball manufacturers at a moderate cost. I&B Chairman Herbert Jaques reports that "public opinion is slowly but surely accepting the fact that only through wise control of the ball can the present length of courses and the playing of them be kept in the proper ratio, and the results of this research now make it possible to establish standards which can be maintained on a permanent basis."

**1929**  Agreed in UK and USA that a ball 1.68 inches in size and 1.55 ounces in weight is best suited for all conditions of play. These standards would be incomplete without including a resilience test, so. no action was taken and they continued to experiment on the Thomas machine. Independent tests carried out by Dr. L.J. Briggs, Director of the Bureau of Standards in Washington, D.C., correspond with results obtained by Professor Thomas. Meetings held with newly formed Golf Ball Manufacturers Association (GBMA).

R&A Rules Committee declares steel shafts to be conforming.

**1930** New standard golf ball adopted by the USGA in April, measuring not less than 1.68" in diameter and weighing not more than 1.55 ounces avoirdupois, effective for play in January 1931. (The R&A never shifted from its 1.62/1.62 ball; its Rules of Golf Committee was also uninterested in the USGA's resilience machine, stating, "The pleasure of playing the game must not be sacrificed to the curtailment of length.")

The concave-face is barred as of January 1, 1931; a rule is added stating that "club faces shall not embody any degree of concavity or more than one angle of loft."

**1931** USGA committee disapproves face markings in the Ruffex iron that had been approved by the R&A. Tests were being conducted on the sandwedge niblick to determine the action of the ball on the clubface.

The lighter, larger "balloon ball" adopted by the USGA (1.68 inches/1,55 ounces) is almost universally despised, and the USGA responds by raising the minimum weight to 1.62 ounces, effective January 1, 1932.

The USGA bans the concave-faced sand wedge, concerned that it strikes the ball twice during a swing.

With his victory at Inverness Club in Toledo, Ohio, Billy Burke becomes the first player to win the U.S. Open using steel-shafted clubs. He defeats George Von Elm by a single stroke in their epic 72-hole play-off.

**1932** Gene Sarazen wins the British and U.S. Opens using his version of a sand wedge, having soldered a flange onto the sole of a wedge. New design is neither concave nor more than one angle of loft.

A regulation approved limiting the use of a rubber-socket joint to one point only in the assembly of a steel-shaft club.

Plywood shafts are approved by the R&A, which had never been barred from USGA championships.

Steel shaft hexagonal in cross section approved.

Shock absorbers under grip permitted.

USGA rules that insets in faces of irons clubs are not allowed.

Wooden weight-adjustable heads permitted as long as they cannot be adjusted after they leave the shop.

**1934**  Significant change in presentation of Rules. New first paragraph declares, "The Game of Golf consists in a ball being played from the 'Teeing Ground' into the 'Hole' by successive strokes, with Clubs and Balls made in conformity with the directions laid down in Clause on 'Form and Make of Golf Clubs and Balls.'" (First time "Form and Make" Clause is explicitly incorporated into the rules; first inclusion of balls with clubs.)

Form and Make Clause now includes the following:

1.  The head of a club shall be so constructed that the length of the head from the back of the heel to the toe shall be greater than the breadth from the face to the back of the head.

2.  The shaft shall be fixed at the heel or to a neck, socket or hose in line with the heel or to a point opposite the heel, either to the right or left, when the club is soled in the ordinary position for play.

3.  The shaft of a putter may be fixed at any point in the head between the heel and a line terminating at the center of the sole.

WEIGHT AND SIZE OF BALL

The weight of the ball shall not be greater than 1.62

ounces avoirdupois, and the size not less than 1.68 inches in diameter. The rules of golf committee and the executive committee of the USGA will take whatever steps they think is necessary to limit the power of the ball with regard to distance should any ball of greater power be introduced.

**1936** Last USGA championship won by a golfer using hickory shafts (Johnny Fischer, U.S. Amateur).

National driving contest held as prelude to the PGA Championship: Sam Snead outdrives Jimmy Thomson with an average of 307 yards for three drives. .

**1937** USGA adopts rule stating that the game of golf shall be played with no more than fourteen clubs beginning January 1, 1938.

After tests of golf ball weight and size and additional tests on flight and roll, USGA informs golf ball manufacturers in a meeting on June 5 that it views with alarm the increasing flight of balls during the past few years. Each manufacturer present promises they will not bring out a ball of greater distance than those already on the market without first notifying the USGA in writing. In addition, they say they will forward copies of their flight tests as they are made.

**1939** R&A adopts fourteen-club limit.

**1941** Manufacturing specifications governing the scoring permitted on the face of a club are developed and distributed to golf club manufacturers in the U.S., such specs to take effect on January 1, 1942. (The specifications required V-shaped grooves and a "land-to-groove" ratio of 3:1.)

USGA issues a decision regarding grip thickness, finding a grip that is 1 3/16-inch to be too thick, despite having previously approved a one-inch grip. This decision set a de facto standard, though it was not written into the Rules of Golf.

I&B Committee hires a technical expert from the Armour Institute of Technology to advise it on equipment issues.

The USGA develops a machine for measuring the initial velocity of a golf ball at impact, with testing conducted by the Armour Institute. Any plans to implement a new rule limiting initial velocity are put on hold until after the War.

**1942**   Paragraph added to the "Form and Make of Clubs and Balls" clause: "(Specifications have been issued to manufacturers. Players in doubt as to the legality of their iron clubs are advised to consult the U.S.G.A.. or manufacturers.)"

Specifications for balls beyond size and weight added to the Rules: "The velocity of the ball shall be not greater than 250 feet per second when measured on the U.S.G.A's apparatus; the temperature of the ball when so tested shall be 75 degrees Fahrenheit; a maximum tolerance of 2% will be allowed on any ball in such velocity test." First performance standard for equipment; first reference to testing in the rules.

Manufacturers are advised to submit "unusual clubs or clubs they thought might be border-line" to the USGA for approval before going into production.

The U.S. government halts the manufacturing of golf equipment.

**1943**   Golf ball machine testing is shut down because of war. New golf ball production is halted; the only manufacture is of reprocessed balls, which traveled nearly as far as new balls.

All applications for approval of clubs must be accompanied by a full size model.

**1947**  Armour Research Foundation in Chicago resumes ball testing.

First rule on grips added, under the heading "Rules Governing Form and Make of Golf Clubs and Balls." "The grip shall consist of a plain extension of the shaft to which material may be added for the purpose of obtaining a firmer hold." Explicit ban on adjustable elements in clubs added to the rules: "A club shall be one unit. All its various parts shall be permanently fixed. No part may be movable or separable or capable of adjustment by the player."

**1948**  Additional wording added to the grip rule: "The grip shall be substantially straight and plain in form, may have flat sides, but may not have a channel* or a furrow* for the fingers or be molded to the fingers. *The above prohibition against a channel or a furrow for the fingers will not become effective until January 1, 1949."

**1949**  PGA and USGA purchase expensive "micrometer microscopes" to measure markings on face of clubs.

Distance measuring device submitted and disapproved. I&B Committee believes such devices are part of an "attempt to short-cut the way to skillful golf."

**1950**  A new, more accurate torsion scale purchased for weighing golf balls. Based on tests conducted at association competitions, one brand was found to be consistently overweight. USGA made contact with the manufacturer, who immediately corrected the situation.

I&B Committee considers adding a limit on compression to the specs for the golf ball.

Approval given to clubfaces with a convex bulge from top to bottom. Clause declaring that a club's face may not have more than one angle of loft is deleted. Concavity is still prohibited.

**1952**  First joint issuance of rules by USGA and R&A, standardizing the rules around the world (with some lingering areas of disagreement). R&A agrees to eliminate the stymie and its ban on center-shafted putters, holds onto its smaller 1.62/1.62 ball.

Little else of substance was changed, but the equipment rules were brought into the main body of the Rules of Golf for the first time, as Rule 2: The Club and the Ball, with subheadings of Legal Clubs and Balls, Form and Make of Clubs, and Weight, Size and Velocity of Ball.

**1953**  Complete specifications for markings on iron clubs listed, with diagrams, in Rules for the first time. Specifications had previously been issued to manufacturers but not published.

Diagrams demonstrating permitted and nonconforming grips added to the back of the rule book.

**1956**  Several revisions to Rule 2-2, Form and Make of Clubs. Purpose of changes, according to USGA's I&B Chairman Charles B. Grace, was "to incorporate interpretations previously issued as decisions and to enunciate the intent of the Rule with greater clarity." The changes: Preamble added: "The United States Golf Association and the Royal and Ancient Golf Club of St. Andrews, Scotland, reserve the right to change the Rules and the interpretations regarding clubs and balls at any time."

New clause 2-2a., General Conditions: "The golf club shall be composed of a shaft and a head, and all of the various parts shall be fixed so that the club is one unit. The club shall not be substantially different from the traditional and customary form and make." (Reference to "contrivances such as springs" has been removed.)

Under MOVABLE PARTS PROHIBITED (now 2-2b.), sentence added: "The player or other agency shall not change the playing characteristics of a club during a round." Clubs with more than one face designed for striking the ball are banned. Exception is made for a putter "if the loft of both faces is practically the same."

Addition made under 2-2f. Grip: "A device designed to give the player artificial aid in gripping and swinging the club shall be deemed to violate this Rule even though it be not a part of the club.

Fiberglass insert in the shaft of a putter approved. By decision, the USGA rescinds its 1941 decision that created a de facto maximum thickness for grips.

**1957**  USGA hires Arthur D. Little, Inc., a research firm, to make a comprehensive study of the golf ball with the possible objects of developing an improved standard or rule to control distance, considering factors beyond initial velocity such as the coefficient of restitution of the ball and aerodynamic forces on the ball in flight. Charles L. Peirson, I&B Chairman, reported the belief that "(i)f there has been a progressive increase in distance or if there is a reasonable possibility of one in the future, it will injure the game by minimizing the premium on control in shotmaking and nullifying the architectural values in courses."

Ball-testing apparatus moved to Golf House.

**1959**  I&B Committee expands to include, as consulting members, four individuals with technical/research backgrounds, including two research engineers and a dean of a school of engineering.

New golf ball testing apparatus received from Arthur D. Little Inc. and installed at "Golf House"

USGA purchased an outdoor golf ball driving machine from the MacNeill Engineering Co. of Waltham, Mass. This was installed at Winged Foot Golf Club. U.S. Testing Company was commissioned to conduct independent testing using this machine to examine the claims being made by manufacturers regarding their golf ball performance.

**1960**  I&B Chairman Clarence W. Benedict reported on the results of the 1959 independent tests by U.S. Testing Company at Winged Foot and stated, "(C)laims concerning distance qualities led us to authorize the United States Testing Co., of Hoboken, NJ, to conduct independent tests…. As a result of these tests, it is the Association's view that no brand of golf ball is appreciably superior to its several nearest competitors in distance qualities."

Rule 37-9, Artificial Devices, added to rule book: "the player shall not use any artificial device for the purpose of gauging or measuring distance or conditions which might affect his play."

**1962**  U.S. Testing Company commissioned to conduct testing of golf balls because it was becoming too technical for USGA staff and committee members who had previously conducted the tests.

**1963**  James Bartsch applies for patent on a solid, one-piece golf ball.

**1964** First inclusion in the Rules of a definition for the words "wood," "iron," and "putter." In Rule 2-2a. General Characteristics: "An 'iron' club is one with a head which usually is relatively narrow from face to back and usually is made of steel. A 'wood' club is one with a head relatively broad from face to back, and usually is made of wood, plastic or a light metal. A 'putter' is a club designed primarily for use on the putting green."

The method of measuring the length and breadth of a clubhead and the distance between the axis of the shaft and the back of the heel made more specific in Rule 2-2c.

**1965** Gary Player is first to win U.S. Open using fiberglass shafts

**1966** The use of Vaseline or other similar substances on clubfaces, before or during a round, was disapproved by ruling.

**1967** Spalding markets the first solid (one-piece) ball under the name "Unicore." It also introduces a version with a polyurethane covering (the first two-piece ball), called the "Executive."

R&A creates an I&B Committee separate from the Rules of Golf Committee; it had always been a subcommittee, but was spun off in December, with the Rules Committee noting, "It will be patent, particularly to those who know or have read the work done in the past on experiments and tests of various balls, that the study of this subject is not for amateurs."

Ram introduces the first golf ball with a cover made of Surlyn, a synthetic material made by Dupont that is far more durable than the traditional balata cover.

**1968**   In quadrennial rules review, several changes made for clarification purposes, effective in 1968:

- Club may not be designed to be adjustable (added to 2-2a, General Characteristics)

- 2-2b, Movable Parts Prohibited was rewritten as Playing Characteristics Not to Be Changed: "The playing characteristics of a club shall not be purposely changed during a round; foreign material shall not be added to the club face at any time."

- Regarding clubfaces, the paragraph dealing with lines and dots is expanded to include "any type of finish, for the purpose of unduly influencing the movement of the ball" (no longer just spin).

- Shaft must be designed to be straight and generally circular in cross-section. Any neck or socket must not be more than 5 inches in length. Exceptions for putters include that the shaft or neck may be fixed at any point in the head, not merely the heel; the axis of the shaft must divert from vertical by at least 10 degrees; shaft in cross-section shall be generally circular or otherwise symmetrical.

- Straddle-putting is banned.

- Under 2-2f, Grip, language added to note that a plain glove is permissible and not considered an artificial aid.

- Foreign material may not be applied to the ball for the purpose of changing its playing characteristics.

- Grooves on the face of an iron club must be straight.

- Rule 37-9, Artificial Devices, expanded to explicitly bar the use of any artificial device "which might assist (the player) in making a stroke or in his play."

British PGA begins a three-year trial of the 1.68-inch ball, signaling a possible move to eliminate the size differences between American and British balls.

Illinois Tool Works machine completed to test COR. New machine to be known as "golf ball test machine-ITW." Purpose was to develop a new multiple impact rule to control performance of golf balls at a variety of impacts. New multiple impact rule was to replace velocity regulation, but it was never adopted.

Periodic testing took place on the MacNeill outdoor testing machine, which can be adjusted to test balls of different sizes. This machine compared carry and roll of one ball with the carry and roll of another. Testing diameters of golf ball (1.68, 1.62, experimental 1.65 ball) as part of joint committee with R&A seeking a uniform ball.

**1969**   The graphite shaft is invented by Frank Thomas as Chief Design engineer for Shakespeare Sporting Goods.

**1970**   Joint committee of the R&A and USGA announce intention to adopt a standard ball with a minimum diameter of 1.66 inches, maximum weight of 1.62 ounces, and maximum initial velocity of 250 feet per second on a standard ball-testing apparatus, along with other possible specifications "as may be determined from time to time."

**1971**   USGA acquires True Temper shaft and club testing machine (Iron Byron).

Alan Shepard hits a golf ball on the moon with a 6-iron.

**1972**   Clubs may be designed to be adjustable in weight, though playing characteristics may not be changed during a round.

If a putter has two faces, the loft must be substantially the same and may not exceed ten degrees.

Wood clubs with lofts of greater than 24 degrees (approximately that of a 5-wood) must conform to the specifications regarding markings on the faces of iron clubs. Other wood clubs have no restriction on the marking designs.

Any inserted plug in a shaft must be generally circular in cross-section; shaft and any included plug must extend to the upper end of the grip. Grip defined in the Rules as "that part of the shaft designed to be held by the player and any material added to it for the purpose of obtaining a firm hold." A device designed to give the player artificial aid in gripping the club is a violation even though it not be part of the grip. (Exceptions: Plain gloves and material or substance applied to the grip, such as tape, gauze or resin.)

USGA indicates to the R&A that it is unlikely to go ahead with the 1.66-inch ball at this time, due to objections from manufacturers and professional players. British PGA decides to continue using the 1.68 ball.

**1973**   Face roughness standard developed by USGA in conjunction with manufacturers.

U.S. manufacturers propose that the 1.66-inch ball be phased in over a ten-to-fifteen-year period.

**1974**   Uniform ball proposal abandoned.

R&A requires use of the 1.68-inch ball in the Open Championship as a Condition of Competition.

USGA appoints Frank Thomas as its first technical director.

**1975**   R&A adopts Initial Velocity standard for balls.

USGA completes Overall Distance Standard for balls, to go into effect March 1, 1976.

**1976**  Revision of Rule 2: The Club and the Ball. Shape of Head, Face of Head, Shaft, and Grip are all moved to Appendix II: Design of Clubs. The Rules themselves were not changed, except for adoption of Overall Distance Standard and reference to R&A adoption of Initial Velocity standard.

Overall Distance Standard, in Rule 2-3a: The Ball, "A brand of golf ball, when tested on apparatus approved by the USGA on the outdoor range at the USGA Headquarters under the conditions set forth in the Overall Distance Standard for golf balls on file with the USGA, shall not cover an average distance in carry and roll exceeding 280 yards, plus a tolerance of 8%. (Note: The 8% tolerance will be reduced to a minimum of 4% as test techniques are improved.)" The ODS, not having been accepted by the R&A, did not apply in international team competitions. (The ODS clause, approved to take effect on March 1, 1976, did not appear in the 1976 Rule Book as published at the start of the year.)

Clause covering Markings on Clubs is now Appendix III, and listed with greater specificity. For irons, reasonably-sized portions of the heel and toe cannot be scored; the width of grooves must be "generally consistent." For woods, decorative markings in the center of the scored area are permitted in a square with sides of .375 inches; such markings may not unduly influence the movement of the ball. If the loft or face angle of a wood is greater than 24 degrees, grooves must be generally straight with a maximum width of .040 inches, and a depth no greater than 1.5 times the width. Distance between the edges of grooves must be no less than three times the width of the adjacent groove. For irons, the degree of decorative sandblasting permitted is not to exceed a roughness of 180 microinches, with 15% tolerance; the direction of measurement will be parallel to the grooves.

If punch marks rather than grooves are used, their area cannot exceed .0044 square inches, may not be closer to another punch mark than 0.168 inches center to center, and depth may not be greater than 0.038 inches. Punch marks must be evenly distributed over the scored area.

**1977**   Testing becomes more sophisticated and detailed, to the point where the data derived can no longer be collated and analyzed by hand. USGA acquires its first minicomputer (Digital PDP 11) to aid its Technical Director and consulting team of eight Ph.Ds.

Polara ball marketed.

USGA discontinues its list of nonconforming balls.

First use of Stimpmeter to measure green speed, redesigned by Frank Thomas. The design is a modification of a device first proposed by Eddie Stimpson in 1935, hence the name.

**1978**   USGA and R&A decide their I&B committees should meet regularly in order to develop uniform standards worldwide.

Polara files lawsuit against the USGA, challenging its nonconforming status.

**1979**   At meetings between R&A and USGA committees during the Walker Cup matches, R&A agrees to appoint a technical consultant who would visit Golf House regularly (all research being conducted by the USGA), and R&A will use USGA ball testing facilities for all 1.68 balls, continuing to use its own contractor for the 1.62 balls.

USGA studies symmetry standard in the wake of the Polara introduction, expects to adopt a new standard in the near future.

Golf Ball Manufacturers Association discontinued.

Gary Adams brings first modern metal-woods (TaylorMade) to market.

**1980** Symmetry standard adopted: "The ball shall be designed and manufactured to perform in general as if it were spherically symmetrical." Extensive detail regarding testing added to Appendix II of the Rules.
Judge Robert Schnacke of the U.S. District Court in California grants summary judgment dismissing antitrust suit filed by the inventors of the Polara ball in 1978. Polara appeals this decision.

**1981** Extensive studies undertaken by USGA in wind tunnel to determine and measure aerodynamic properties of a ball in flight. Goal is to conduct future testing under indoor laboratory conditions, resulting in greater accuracy and reduced cost.

**1982** At the Hawaiian Open, Wayne Levi becomes the first golfer to win a Tour event using an orange ball.

**1983** Equipment rules are modified as part of rules reorganization for 1984 edition. The Rules will cover items the golfer himself can check, while the technical information mainly directed at the manufacturers is moved to the Appendices.

Clubs and The Ball are now Rule 4 and 5 respectively.

- Shaft must have the same general bending and twisting properties in any direction; this replaces the language stating that the shaft must be circular.

- Grip must be generally circular in cross-section, except that it may have a slightly raised, straight rib running the length of the grip. Putter grips may have a noncircular cross-section, so long as there is no concavity and it remains similar throughout the length of the grip. (Previously, flat sides were permitted in any grip, not merely for putters.) The axis of the grip must coincide with the axis of the shaft, except for a putter.

- Distinction between woods and irons is removed from the definition of a club in the Form and Make of Clubs clause. This eliminates the requirement that the face of an iron club must be flat, though it still may have no concavity.

- The clubface must, in relation to the ball, be hard and rigid. In Appendix II, under Hardness and Rigidity, "The club face must not be designed and manufactured to have the effect at impact of a spring which would unduly influence the movement of the ball."

- Grooves other than V-shape are permitted, so long as they have diverging sides and a symmetrical cross-section. The depth of a groove may not exceed .020 inches (0.5 mm).

- Inserts are not permitted on a club that has metal as its basic structural material.

The changes listed in the six paragraphs above are in effect for any clubs manufactured after January 1, 1984. Existing clubs that conformed prior to these changes may be used until December 31, 1989.

USGA develops turfgrass hardness tester (patent issued in 1989).

R&A adopts 1.68 ball for all its championships.

**1984**  USGA Research and Test Center opens, 7200-square foot building designed to house all facilities needed to evaluate equipment, including Iron Byron and an observation deck to accommodate visitors.

Polara antitrust suit goes to trial in U.S. District Court

in San Francisco. Jury finds in October that the USGA conspired with golf ball manufacturers to restrain sales of the Polara ball, awards $1.47 million to Polara (tripled under antitrust law to $4.41 million). In December, Judge Robert Schnacke issues "judgment notwithstanding the verdict" overturning the award, declaring that there was no such conspiracy and the USGA had acted "solely in accordance with its responsibilities to the game of golf."

At the Open Championship, R&A General Committee states that "thought should be given to the matter" of changing minimum diameter of a ball under the Rules from 1.62 inches to 1.68.

Lee Trevino becomes the first player to win a major – PGA Championship – using a metal-headed driver

**1985**   Polara files appeal in January of Judge Schnacke's 1984 ruling. USGA and Polara settle lawsuit in November, USGA paying $1.37 million.

Pelz Research files suit against the USGA over determination that their three-ball putter is nonconforming because its measurement from face to back is greater than from toe to heel.

**1986**   Tolerance in Overall Distance Standard reduced to 6% from 8%. USGA notifies manufacturers that some clubs might not conform due to the rounding of the edges of U-shaped grooves.

Greg Norman becomes the first player to win a major – British Open – using a two-piece ball – the Spalding Tour Edition.

Bob Tway becomes the first player to win a major – PGA Championship – using investment cast irons – Ping Eye2

Pelz lawsuit dropped.

**1987**   USGA announced 30-degree method of measuring the

width of grooves, following an extensive, multiyear study of the effect of V-shaped and U-shaped grooves under fairway and rough conditions. Open hearing is held at Golf House to discuss effect of pending method of measurement. Previously conforming grooves will be permitted in general play until 1996, and in USGA competitions beginning in 1990. Among the clubs affected by this are the Ping Eye2 irons.

Appendix II lists precisely where on the clubhead measurements of width and depth will be made.

If a putter has two faces, they must be opposite each other.

Clause on Damage to Clubs makes explicit that if a club is damaged other than in the normal course of play, it may not be replaced or repaired during the round.

R&A adopts the 1.68-inch ball for all play, effective January 1, 1990.

"Plain in shape" in relation to the clubhead is clarified: "appendages to the main body of the head such as knobs, plates, rods, and fins for the purpose of meeting dimensional specifications…are not permitted." Preamble to the rule is expanded to note, "If a manufacturer fails to [submit a sample club for a ruling on conformity], he assumes the risk of a ruling that the club does not conform with the Rules of Golf."

**1988**   PGA Tour Policy Board announces it will adopt a rule allowing only traditional V-grooves in its events, effective January 1989 – a decision more restrictive than USGA Rules, which permit U-grooves that meet its specifications. USGA urges PGA Tour to reconsider, which it does, pending results of a player test study.

Implements & Ball Committee (I&B) of the USGA changes its name to Equipment Standards Committee.

Square-grooved clubs such as the Ping Eye2 irons are banned by the USGA, which claims that tests show the clubs give an unfair competitive advantage to Ping customers. The PGA Tour also bans the clubs in 1989. Karsten Manufacturing, maker of the clubs, fights a costly two-year battle with both the USGA and the PGA Tour to have the ban rescinded after winning a temporary injunction.

The R&A, after thirty-eight years, adopts the 1.68 inch diameter ball in the revision to take effect in 1990.

**1989** Karsten lawsuit filed in Arizona over nonconforming status of grooves in Ping Eye2 irons. At the Walker Cup Dinner in Atlanta in August, writs are served on the R&A, the USGA, and a number of their officers and employees.

R&A and its officers are dismissed from the Karsten lawsuit, as Arizona court has no jurisdiction over it.

Long putter is permitted. Equipment Standards Committee reports, "This putter was not considered to be a threat to the game, even though the style is somewhat unconventional." Extremely short putter is banned; shaft must be at least 18 inches (457 mm) in length.

**1990** Karsten lawsuit settled.

R&A and USGA will meet twice annually to help expedite process of issuing equipment decisions.

USGA declares Weight-Rite shoes – golf shoes with soles that are 1/8 inch higher on the outside to promote proper footwork in the swing – a violation of Rule 14-3a, which bans artificial or unusual equipment "that might aid [the golfer] in making a stroke or in his play." Weight-Rite sues, seeking an injunction against the ruling; court rules for the USGA on the merits, affirming its authority to make the Rules.

R&A adopts Overall Distance Standard for golf balls.

R&A rule regarding 1.68 inch diameter ball goes into effect. For the first time since 1910, the Rules of Golf are fully standardized throughout the world.

**1991**   USGA's Equipment Standards Committee changes its name back to Implements & Ball Committee.

Indoor Testing Range (ITR) is developed at Golf House to measure the optimum launch conditions of a golf ball.

As a result of USGA research and testing, rule is altered to allow insets of other materials in the faces of iron clubs and metal-woods.

Oversized metal-woods are introduced, with Callaway's Big Bertha quickly establishing itself as the dominant brand; the Big Bertha driver becomes one of the biggest-selling clubs of all time.

**1992**   Putters are made an exception to the rules on adjustability. They may be adjustable other than for weight (already permitted) so long as the adjustment cannot be readily made; the adjustable parts are firmly fixed and unlikely to come loose during a round; all configurations of adjustment conform with the Rules.

Cross-sectional dimension of a grip measured in any direction may not exceed 1.75 inches (45 mm).

A putter may have more than one grip, provided each is circular in cross-section and coincides with the axis of the shaft.

Specifications on impact-area markings on the face of a club do not apply to putters.

**1993**   USGA Test Center becomes fully operational. Research continues on aerodynamics and biomechanics.

SoftSpikes are introduced, in an effort to combat the damage to putting greens caused by traditional metal golf spikes.

Bernhard Langer wins the Masters using a persimmon driver, becoming the last player to win a major with a wooden-headed driver.

**1995**   First titanium drivers hit the market.

**1996**   Specifications for golf ball symmetry are removed from the text of Appendix III-c, intent and effect of the Rule is unchanged.

Preamble to Rule 4 states that "A manufacturer may submit to the United States Golf Association a sample of a club which is to be manufactured …" (Prior preamble alluded to manufacturers submitting if they are in doubt as to conformity; implication now is that everyone should.) Preamble also states, "Where a club, or part of a club, is required to have some specific property, this means that it must be designed and manufactured with the intention of having that property. The finished club or part must have that property within manufacturing tolerances appropriate to the material used." (Codifies intent as being equally important as outcome of product.)

Putter by definition may not have a loft exceeding ten degrees. Specifications on alignment for all clubs are added. Shafts may not be angled more than 20 degrees backward or forward along the line of play. The 10-degree lie specification is expanded to apply to all clubs, not just putters.

Grip may have a slightly indented spiral replicating a wrapped grip. Permitted exceptions for grips within the Artificial Devices rule now include "powder and drying or moisturizing agents" in addition to resin.

Rule 5: The Ball now includes specific reference to

potential Condition of Competition in which the ball used by a player must be named on the List of Conforming Golf Balls issued by the USGA.

Exception for putters is made to the requirement that the face of a club be hard and rigid.

Examples are added to the requirement that a clubhead be "plain in shape," while noting, "It is not practicable to define plain in shape precisely and comprehensively...."

Impact area on clubfaces must be of a single material (exceptions may be made for wooden clubs), and may not include any surface roughness beyond that of decorative sandblasting or fine milling. Restrictions on face markings apply to clubs with faces of a similar hardness to metal, whether actually made of metal or not.

Spalding introduces the Strata golf ball, the first multilayer nonwound golf ball.

**1997**    Research program at USGA begins under the name "B.A.S.I.C." (biomechanics, aerodynamics, shaft, impact, clubhead)

**1998**    USGA limits springlike effect.

**1999**    The USGA begins testing metal-headed drivers for springlike effect.

**2000**    USGA Senior Technical Director of Operations and Equipment Standards John Matheny retires in January. Dick Rugge hired in May as Senior Technical Director. Frank Thomas steps down as Technical Director in October.

R&A announces it will not adopt the USGA's COR limit on springlike effect.

USGA creates a list of conforming drivers, which can be accessed online.

Rule 4: The Club is greatly simplified, with specifications shifted to Appendix II: Design of Clubs. Many specifications or testing protocols – including those for Initial Velocity, Overall Distance Standard, and springlike effect – are not detailed, except by reference to information "on file with the United States Golf Association."

If a putter has split grips, the two grips must be separated by at least 1.5 inches (38.1 mm).

In 14-3: Artificial Devices and Unusual Equipment, an exception that allowed tape or gauze to be added to a grip is removed; they may only be used if the intent is to repair the grip.

**2001**    USGA updates Iron Byron for indoor testing of ODS in conjunction with indoor testing range.

USGA publishes list of conforming golf balls and nonconforming drivers on its website.

**2002**    Publication of the R&A/USGA joint statement of principles.
R&A announces decision to limit springlike effect in drivers to be phased in over a five-year period beginning at the Open Championship in 2003.

**2003**    Pendulum test for springlike effect where a golf ball sized hemisphere impacts the face of a golf club allowing the time of contact to be determined (characteristic time) is developed jointly by R&A and USGA.

New test conditions are proposed for indoor ball tests to incorporate the use of a modern titanium driver head and increased swing speed of 120 mph. This reflects the playing conditions of 2003.

The length of a club (except for putters) may not exceed 48 inches (1,219.2 mm) – first upper limit on clubs.

Clubheads may not be wider than 5 inches (127 mm) from heel to toe, nor taller than 2.8 inches (71.12 mm) from sole to crown. The depth of the clubhead from face to back must be smaller than the width from heel to toe. The overall size of a clubhead may not exceed 28.06 cubic inches (460 cubic centimeters), with a tolerance of 0.61 cubic inches (10 cubic centimeters).

A tee may not be longer than 4 inches

Titliest introduces the solid-core, urethane-covered Pro V1 golf ball, leading to the rapid demise of the wound ball.

**2004**   I&B Committee of the USGA changes its name again to Equipment Standards Committee.

Rules governing the shape and face size for putters with unusually shaped heads are spelled out and clarified in Appendix II.

Overall Distance Standard is redefined to reflect greater clubhead speed of professionals and to incorporate titanium clubface. Clubhead speed is increased to 120 mph, resulting in a revised ODS of 317 yards (with a test tolerance of 1%, for a total ODS of 320 yards).

**2005**   List of conforming driver heads published.

USGA asks manufacturers to develop and submit golf balls that would comply with a reduction in the ODS by either 15 or 25 yards. USGA will study what the effect of such reductions would be on golfers at varying levels of skill.

Devices that measure distance only may be permitted by Local Rule.

Definition of "normal course of play," under which a damaged club may be repaired or replaced during a round, is broadened to include "all reasonable acts" excluding "cases of abuse."

**2007**   USGA and R&A announce first restriction on Moment of Inertia: Woods may not have an MOI component around the vertical axis through the clubhead's center of gravity of greater than 5900 g cm (32.259 oz in), plus a test tolerance of 100 g cm (0.547 oz in). Restriction to be incorporated into 2008 Rules.

**2008**   Restrictions on adjustability are eased somewhat; USGA will allow clubs to be adjustable other than just for weight, subject to review.

Further details added to clarify meaning of "plain in shape" for clubheads. Details have not been in the Rules before, though they were listed in guidelines on equipment rules.

New section on springlike effect: As measured in Pendulum Test Protocol, it now applies to all clubs except putters and in all forms of the game, no longer just a Condition of Competition.

USGA announces revisions to groove rule, reducing the permitted volume of grooves and the sharpness of their edges. The new specifications to take effect as a Condition of Competition in 2010, and for all play in 2024. This is the first equipment rollback in seventy-two years.

**2009**   USGA and R&A issue joint statement on electronic devices, declaring they have no intention of allowing such devices for any purpose other than measuring distance; such other purposes would include measuring wind speed or direction, the slope of the ground, temperature, or any form of advice as to the kind of shot to be played. Neither the USGA nor R&A anticipate adopting the Local Rule permitting such devices at their championships.

**2010**   Groove rule change declared in 2008 goes into effect.

USGA launches Rules application for iPhone and iPod Touch.

USGA publishes a notice to discuss the process used in formulating rules and that it will hold a forum on this subject in fall 2010. All interested parties including manufacturers, players, media, and golf organizations will be invited to participate and make their views on equipment rule-making known to the USGA and each other. The USGA anticipates that this forum will provide input and help the USGA enhance the rule-making process.

In November 2010 this meeting was held, however media and others were not permitted and the discussion took place between the manufacturers and the USGA, with no publication of the proceedings.

## ABOUT THE AUTHORS

**Frank Thomas** inventor of the graphite shaft, has spent much of his life working with and serving as one of the guardians of the game of golf. In his twenty-six years as Technical Director of the United States Golf Association, he was responsible for testing and ruling on the acceptability of every new club, ball, and accessory. He redesigned and introduced the Stimpmeter to the world of golf. Since leaving the U.S.G.A. in 2000, he has devoted his efforts and passion to educating consumers about golf technology and providing them with the information they need to make better decisions about their equipment. His opinions on the game have appeared on the Op-Ed page of *The New York Times*, he comments on and evaluates equipment and issues at his website www.franklygolf.com and is Technical Advisor to various golf media outlets. At the request of and in partnership with the Professional Golfers Association (PGA) of Great Britain and Ireland, he developed an online Certified Putting Instructor course for golf professionals that is endorsed, approved, and recognized by PGAs around the world. Frank is also the author of *Just Hit It* and co-author of *Dear Frank… Answers to 100 of Your Golf Equipment Questions*.

**Valerie Melvin** is the Managing Director and co-founder of Frankly Golf and Frankly Academies, the worldwide leader in putting instruction. She holds a Bachelor's Honours Degree in Psychology from the University of Stirling and a Master's in Medical Science from the University of Glasgow. A former editor of *Golf Science International* (a publication of the World Scientific Congress of Golf), she has represented her native Scotland in international golf. She was the driving force behind the development of Frankly Academies Certified Putting Instructor online course, endorsed by Professional Golfers Associations around the world. Valerie is also co-author of *Dear Frank... Answers to 100 of Your Golf Equipment Questions*. She currently resides in Celebration, Florida.